Simple Dreams

A Musical Memoir

Linda Ronstadt

Simon & Schuster
New York London Toronto Sydney New Delhi

Simon & Schuster
1230 Avenue of the Americas
New York, NY 10020

First Simon & Schuster hardcover edition September 2013

SIMON & SCHUSTER and colophon are registered trademarks of Simon & Schuster, Inc.

"Long Long Time": Words and music by Gary White © Universal Music Corporation. Reproduced by permission of Hal Leonard.

"Heart Like a Wheel": Words and music by Anna McGarrigle © Anna McGarrigle Music. Administered by Kobalt Music Publishing America, Inc. Reproduced by permission of Kobalt Music.

"Still Within the Sound of My Voice": Words and music by Jimmy Webb © Seventh Son Music, Inc., c/o Music of Windswept and Bug Music, Inc. Reproduced by permission of Hal Leonard.

Photos are from the author's collection unless otherwise noted.

For information about special discounts for bulk purchases, please contact Simon & Schuster Special Sales at 1-866-506-1949 or business@simonandschuster.com.

The Simon & Schuster Speakers Bureau can bring authors to your live event. For more information or to book an event, contact the Simon & Schuster Speakers Bureau at 1-866-248-3049 or visit our website at www.simonspeakers.com.

Designed by John Kosh with Nancy Singer

Manufactured in the United States of America

10 9 8 7 6 5 4 3

Library of Congress Cataloging-in-Publication Data
Ronstadt, Linda.
Simple dreams : a musical memoir / Linda Ronstadt.
pages   cm
Includes index.
1. Ronstadt, Linda. 2. Singers—United States—Biography.
I. Title.
ML420.R8753A3   2013
782.42164092—dc23   2013009309
[B]

ISBN 978-1-4516-6872-8
ISBN 978-1-4516-6874-2 (ebook)

For Mary and Carlos

Truth is simple, but seldom ever seen
Let nothing come between simple man, simple dream.

—John David Souther, "Simple Man, Simple Dream"

Amo, lloro, canto, sueño. (I love, I cry, I sing, I dream.)

—Rafael Bolívar Coronado and Pedro Elías Gutiérrez,
"Alma Llanera"

Contents

Contents

Simple Dreams

Smiling at our big tomcat in the dress my mother made for my first day of school.

1

Tucson

ON HER WAY TO the hospital the day I was born, my mother wanted to stop and eat a hamburger. She was hungry, and maybe wanted to fortify herself against the brutally hard work of pushing out a baby, a task that lay immediately and ominously before her. It was raining hard, and the streets were badly flooded. My father, a prudent man, wanted to be sure I was born in the hospital and not in his car. He loved my mother tenderly and was unlikely to deny her anything within reason, but he denied her this, and so I was delivered safely from the watery world of her interior to the watery exterior world of the Arizona desert in a cloudburst.

In the desert, rain is always a cause for jubilation. July and August brought the ferocious seasonal rainstorms on which all life, including mine, depended.

I was brought home to a house my parents had built of adobe on the last ten acres of my grandfather Fred Ronstadt's cattle ranch. He had sold it off in parcels during the dunning years of the Depression and relied on the thriving hardware business he had built in downtown Tucson at the end of the nineteenth century to supply a living for my grandmother and their four sons. It bore his name proudly as the F. Ronstadt Hardware Company and took up nearly a city block. I remember it as a wonderful place of heavily timbered floors and the pervasive smell of diesel oil. Inside it were tractors, bulldozers, pumps, windmills, bins of nails, camping supplies, high quality tools, and housewares.

My grandfather, having been born in Sonora, Mexico, did business with all the Mexican ranchers who were within a three or four days' drive by car, a journey often made by my father. In those days, the border was a friendly place, and easy to cross. We knew many of the families in the north of Mexico, and we attended one another's balls, picnics, weddings, and baptisms. My parents often drove us across the border into Nogales, which had wonderful stores where we would shop. After that, they would take us to the cool, plush recesses of the Cavern Café, and we would be served a delicious turtle soup.

I deeply miss those times when the border was a permeable line and the two cultures mixed in a natural and agreeable fashion. Lately, the border seems more like the Berlin Wall, and functions mainly to separate families and interfere with wildlife migration.

My father, in addition to working in the hardware store and going to the University of Arizona in Tucson, helped my grandfather on the ranches he owned.

My mother, who was called Ruth Mary, told us that the first time she saw my father, he was riding his horse up the stairs of her sorority house. He was pursuing someone who was not my mother, but his eye was soon drawn to her.

In 1934 she'd made the three-day journey by train from her home state of Michigan to the University of Arizona, where she was enrolled to study math and physics. She was passionate about math. When she was worried or couldn't sleep, we would find her at three o'clock in the morning, sitting at the dining room table, working a problem in calculus.

Her father was Lloyd G. Copeman, a well-known inventor, with the electric toaster, electric stove, rubber ice cube tray, and pneumatic grease gun to his credit. He also operated an experimental dairy farm in the Michigan countryside and, early in the twentieth century, invented a milking machine. He used to demonstrate one of his inventions, a 1918 version of the microwave oven that he called "cold heat," by frying an egg through a newspaper. Thinking that the oven was too expensive to manufacture, he never patented it. He worked closely with Charles Stewart Mott, then chairman of the board of General Motors, and developed a great deal of what was then state-of-the-art equipment in the Buick factory in Flint, Michigan.

Old Mr. Mott was fond of my mother and came many times to visit us in the wilds of Tucson. In the fifties, he was caricatured with his enormously bushy white eyebrows as General Bullmoose in *Li'l Abner*, a long-running comic strip drawn by Al Capp. We read it regularly in the *Tucson Daily Citizen*.

Coming from such a background, my mother must have found my father, and the Arizona desert that had shaped him, to be richly exotic.

My father, known as Gilbert, was handsome and somewhat shy. He rarely spoke unless he had something worthy to say. When he did speak, his words carried a quiet authority. He had a beautiful baritone singing voice that sounded like a cross between Pedro Infante, the famous Mexican matinee idol and singer, and Frank Sinatra. He often sang at local venues like the Fox Tucson Theatre, where he was billed as Gil Ronstadt and his Star-Spangled Megaphone. He serenaded my mother under her window with pretty Mexican songs such as "La Barca de Oro" and "Quiéreme Mucho." Added to this was the fact that when my mother was introduced to my grandfather, an autodidact, he dazzled her with his knowledge of geometry and calculus. My mother surely thought she was marrying into a gene pool that would produce mathematicians, but my grandfather was also a musician, so musicians were what she got.

In the late nineteenth century, my grandfather was the conductor of a brass band called the Club Filarmónico Tucsonense. He taught people how to play their instruments, conducted the band, composed and arranged, and played the flute. I have the cornet part written in his own hand from an instrumental arrangement he wrote for *The Pirates of Penzance* in 1896.

He was a widower when he married my grandmother. A daughter from his first marriage, Luisa Espinel, was a singer, dancer, and music scholar who collected and performed traditional songs and dances from northern Mexico and many regions in Spain. She can be seen in a brief comedic appearance as a Spanish dancer in *The Devil Is a Woman*, a 1935 film that starred Marlene Dietrich.

In the twenties, she wrote a letter home to my grandfather from Spain, where she had been performing. In it she reported that she was hugely excited about a guitarist she had hired to be her accompanist. She said he was such a brilliant player that he could hold the audience when she left the stage to change costumes. She wanted to bring him to the United States because she was sure he would make a huge hit with American audiences and eventually establish his own career. His name was Andrés Segovia.

When we were small children, visits from Aunt Luisa were wonderfully exciting. She taught my sister how to do the shimmy and how to play the castanets, and allowed her to try on the beautiful regional Spanish costumes that she had worn as a dancer.

She had lived many years in Spain and been married to a painter who was a Communist and had supported the cause to establish a republic in the Spanish Civil War. My aunt had been friends with the poet Federico García Lorca, who used to play her guitar while he recited his beautiful poems. We found her deliriously glamorous. Many years later, I would take the title of a collection of Mexican folk songs and stories she published called *Canciones de Mi Padre*, and use it to title my own first recording of traditional Mexican songs.

My mother and father married in 1937. Between that time and the beginning of World War II, they produced my sister, Suzy, and my brother Peter.

When the war started and my father joined the army, our mother went to work at night in the control tower of Davis-Monthan Army Air Field, the base outside of Tucson. Toward the end of the war, the planes that flew out of there on their way to war were mostly brand-new Boeing B-29 Superfortresses. After the war was over, all but a few of the B-29s that could still fly came back to Davis-Monthan, part of which became a graveyard for the decommissioned planes of World War II. Their flight path took them directly over our house. My mother would catch the sound of their engines and run outside and wave at them frantically. We kids would wave too. She had launched them into battle from her control tower, and she must have felt some obligation and no small amount of emotion to welcome home the ones that made it back alive.

I was steeped in the sound of the B-29s in my childhood and often tried to emulate it in the string arrangements in my recordings. It seems to appear in the grind between the cello and double bass, particularly in the interval of a fifth.

In the treacherous currents of the Great Depression and World War II, my grandfather nearly lost his hardware business. His unwillingness to foreclose on the farmers and ranchers who were struggling in the same way didn't help his bottom line, but he was loved and respected throughout the valley and beyond to Mexico as a good man who kept his word.

During the Depression, my father turned down an offer from Paul Whiteman, by far the most popular bandleader of his time, to tour with them as their "boy singer." Over the years, other singers with the Whiteman Orchestra included Bing Crosby, Mildred Bailey, and Billie Holiday. I believe it was a decision that caused him some disappointment, but family loyalties prevailed. He and his brothers helped my grandfather with the ranch and the hardware store, finally selling off the ranch and plowing the money back into the store. They managed to survive the Depression and build the business.

There was never any extra cash, but we had what we needed. My mother used to joke that when she first met my father, he had a red convertible, a horse, a ranch, and a guitar. After she married him, all he had left was the guitar. He had my mother too. They rarely quarreled, and when they did, it was well out of earshot of their children. They were always on each other's side, and their marriage lasted until my mother died in 1982.

Newcomers to the desert are shocked when I suggest to them that the most dangerous thing in it is not the poisonous Gila monster or the sidewinder rattlesnake that also makes its home there. It is water. Water is not quick to be absorbed into the hard-packed desert floor. Instead, it runs all over the surface of the ground and reflects the gray clouds that temporarily mask the pitiless heat and glare of the summer sun. This gives the sky and ground a silvery luminosity that is particular to desert landscapes, and transforms the desert itself into something that looks like a delicate construct of shimmering Venetian glass.

Sometimes water can get trapped behind brush and debris that has blocked a dry streambed or arroyo, and when the pressure becomes more than the brush dam can bear, a flash flood is the result. The water takes on the appearance of a twisting, angry animal. The sound alone could scare you to death. There are huge boulders being rolled along at the bottom, making a menacing, growling rumble, and then the roar of the rushing wall of water, which can contain anything from huge logs to sections of some rancher's fence—even his pickup truck.

As very young children, we were warned to head immediately for high ground if there was any sign of rain on the horizon. We knew not to linger in the usually dry rivers and washes where we would spend hours hunting for sand rubies, Indian pottery shards, or maybe even gold. My father had taught us how to use a shallow pan and patiently wash the sand until you "get a little color." The earth in Arizona is so mineral rich that sometimes we did see something glinting in the pan, but not very often and not enough to make us rich too.

It was hot work moving around in the desert. We often went barefoot, but the ground in summer would become so hot that it could raise a blister. The remedy for this was to wet our feet, then dip them in the dry, powdery clay dust, then a little wet mud, and then back into the dust again until we had built up layers of earth to insulate us from the heat. We called this making "mud huaraches," or sandals. It was very effective. If one weren't near a convenient hose or puddle, one simply ran from shade to shade, which seemed to exist in a sadistically meager quantity. The minute we were tall enough to climb onto the back of a horse, we added yet another layer to cushion us from the punishing hot ground.

The first thing I remember ever really wanting, besides the close proximity of my parents, was a horse. My desire for a horse was as fierce as hunger and thirst. I stared at pictures of them in my little books, and drew and colored them with my pencils and crayons—usually colors like pale turquoise, lavender, and rosy pink, and not the more prosaic buckskin, bay, and sorrel colors that I observed on the hides of real horses.

There was one little girl, two years my senior, who lived near enough to visit. One of eight children, her name was Dana, and she was friendly, smart, and had the thing I yearned for most, which was a pony of her own. Her pony was spotted black and white, his name was Little Paint, and a saintlier beast has never been born. Shetland ponies are often mischievous and can be quite naughty, bucking and biting and refusing to budge for their tiny riders. Who can blame them after all that we make them do, encumbering them with saddles and rigid metal bits and then expecting them to haul us around in the hot Arizona sun?

Little Paint, a Shetland crossbred with the more sweet-natured and slightly bigger Welsh pony, was a perfect gentleman. Since there was only one of him, Dana and I would clamber up on his round back and ride double. He was a sturdy little fellow and bore us uncomplainingly wherever we bade him. We would also hitch him up to Dana's pony cart, and he would pull us alongside the blacktop road all the way to the Fort Lowell drugstore, which had a soda fountain. It was like having a car at age four.

I began to beg my parents for a pony of my own, drooping around the house and visibly pining, hinting that without a pony I might not be expected to live. It being within months of my fifth birthday, my father, showing true mercy, decided to buy me a pony. In those days, this could be done for surprisingly little money.

Dana's father operated a small farm nearby and was also a photographer. He photographed people's children dressed up in a cowboy suit and mounted on Little Paint. He had a second pony who had not been a successful picture pony—most likely because he was all Shetland and less patient with the business of having cowboy-suited tots loaded on and off his back all day. His name was Murphy, Dana's last name being O'Sullivan.

Murphy was small and black, and with his shaggy winter coat, he looked exactly like a giant caterpillar. I fell in love with him immediately. My father made arrangements with Mr. O'Sullivan, and Murphy came home to live with us.

He was somewhat ill tempered and used to dump me off his back and run home, work the lid off the galvanized steel can where we kept his oats, and commence to eat his dinner. I would find him there chewing away after I hiked back, beet red in the face from the heat and the mortification of having him buck me off. I retaliated by taking Murphy inside our house, much cooler than his stable, and feeding him ice cream.

Sometimes he would wriggle under the wire fence of his enclosure and cross blacktop roads humming with traffic to find the nearest subdivision, where one fellow grew a clover lawn. This was much tastier than the Bermuda grass we grew on our lawn. The owner of the clover lawn, much annoyed, would call my mother. Everyone in the vicinity knew Murphy and where he lived. My mother drove a 1951 Chevrolet sedan that she named Frank & Earnest. She would remove the backseat, drive to the subdivision with the clover lawn, squeeze Murphy into the vacant anterior recess of Frank & Earnest, and drive home with Murphy cheerfully taking in the sights, his head hanging out the window. My mother then gave him fresh carrots from her vegetable garden, sugar lumps, and corn husks, which he ate with relish. In summer I would gather mesquite beans by the gunnysackful and load them into his manger. We both loved eating the mesquite beans, which are sweet as candy, packed with nutrients, and will fatten a horse and make its coat shine better than oats will. During the rainy season, I would lead Murphy in his halter to the sweet grasses that grew in the ditches watered by the runoff. He continued to dump me on the ground whenever he got tired of carrying me. We were inseparable.

Dana and I would saddle up in the mornings and meet half the distance between our houses, and then ride to the nearby Rillito River. This river was bone dry most of the year, so we used to slide our ponies down one steep side and then scramble up the equally steep opposite side. Now we were in the foothills of the Catalina Mountains, at that time completely devoid of the greedy and cynical development that continues to chip away at its beauty and uniqueness.

The place where I grew up bore no resemblance whatsoever to the pictures in the little books I read as a child. I wondered what kind of a place would have such an abundance of lollipop trees and lush green meadows that didn't even have to be watered with a hose. Instead, we had the giant cacti known as saguaros. These enormous plant beings (I can think of no other way to describe them) grow within a few hundred miles of Tucson and no place else on the face of the earth. They are the cleverest of water hoarders and can expand their leathery green skin to capture as much as a ton of additional water. Saguaros produce an extravagantly voluptuous white blossom, which is the bravest gesture I can imagine in an environment so purely hostile to plant growth.

Everything in the desert seems to either want to inject one with venom or give a vicious stab with a thorn, but we were rarely injured in this manner. I prefer to think that we were lovingly protected by the great good sense and vigilant valor of Murphy and Little Paint. I remember Paint skidding to a halt one afternoon at the sight of a huge rattlesnake stretched across the trail in front of us.

Our parents expected us to be home by dark, and we had no

reason to dawdle, as a place with so many spines and fangs was no place we wanted to be after sundown. The trip home always seemed to take half the time, because Murphy and Little Paint were eager for their dinner. We clung like burrs on their backs and rode like the wind. We were eager for our dinner too.

The year before Murphy came into our lives, my mother had brought home a brown and white springer spaniel puppy. She called him "His Honor the Judge" because his curly ears reminded her of the wigs worn in the British court. One late afternoon, we were cruising down the road in Frank & Earnest, Mother driving and the puppy with me in the backseat. Some exuberant canine impulse caused His Honor to jump from the backseat into her lap. This had the unhappy effect of landing us in the ditch that ran by the side of the road. My mother was very calm. I remember her saying "Well! Here we are!" in a chipper voice and then climbing out of the car so she could pull me out of the back. My knees were skinned, but neither of us seemed to be seriously hurt, so we hiked to the nearest gas station, and someone came and took us home.

The following morning, my mother leaned over the sink to brush her teeth. Next, she was lying on the floor and couldn't move her legs. Again, she stayed calm, so I wasn't aware that anything was particularly wrong. My father was helping her, and he was pretty calm too.

Eventually some men arrived with a tidy little bed on wheels, loaded my mother on it, and wheeled her out the door and into an ambulance. I was fascinated by the little bed with its crisp sheets and neatly tucked-in blanket, and hoped I'd get a turn on it next. I fully expected her to be right back after a short ride around the neighborhood. I thought I would spend the morning helping her to make beds and hang wet clothes on the line, rake leaves, feed the chickens, and gather the eggs. My mother still wasn't around at bedtime, and she didn't read to me from her own childhood collection of the Oz books by L. Frank Baum, which were my favorites. She didn't turn up the next morning at breakfast, either, and by now I'd gathered that she wasn't feeling well and had ridden in that little bed to St. Mary's Hospital. I knew about this place because my older brother had been hit by a car and taken to the hospital with a broken leg. They put a cast on the leg, and we went there and brought him home. My sister had been treated for polio at the hospital, but she came home too, and she was fine. I didn't know what was wrong with my mother or when we would bring her home. I didn't know that she was completely paralyzed from the waist down and not expected to walk ever again.

A thin-lipped, rather severe woman of Scottish extraction who wore a green-striped uniform was moved into our guesthouse. She had been hired to care for me; my sister, Suzy; and my brother, Peter; keep the house clean; and do the cooking. No wonder she was grouchy. We thought her cooking tasted funny. She fried steaks in a pan until they were gray and rubbery. She introduced us to Jell-O. I wasn't in school yet, so I was home with her by myself all day. With all that she had to do, she understandably paid me very little attention. I learned to entertain myself. I spent hours pretending that I was galloping with Hopalong Cassidy and his big white stallion, Topper, chasing cattle rustlers. Hoppy and I were tight. We did everything together.

I figured out how to work the big combination radio–record player and would twist the dial through the Arizona call letters beginning with K. Also, I could get the Mexican stations, beginning with X. They played blaring mariachi *rancheras:* accordion-driven polkas, waltzes, and *corridos* from the mighty state of Sonora. *¡Sí, señor!*

This was before rock and roll, and I listened to the sonic fantasies of a country still reeling from the war, with men finally home from the nightmares they had endured and survived, and wouldn't talk about. The songs were all about pleasant, positive things: love and marriage, doggies in the window, counting blessings.

My father had some 78 rpm recordings, and I liked those better. Bizet's *Carmen*, Grieg's *Peer Gynt*, and the flamenco singer Pastora Pavón, known as La Niña de los Peines, who sang in a slangy Spanish that I couldn't understand. She killed me. I could somehow sense that she was not singing about something pleasant, she was singing about something essential. Something she yearned for so much it burned her, like I felt when I missed my mother, which was all the time.

The Scottish woman had not been raised in the desert, so she wasn't going for the mud huaraches. She insisted that I wear my little black patent leather party shoes, which I wore only to birthday parties and had already outgrown. They pinched my toes and rubbed my heels to blisters, which I popped with a pin. They hurt like hell. I couldn't stand shoes for years after that and still always buy them a size too big. The Scottish woman, who apparently wasn't aware that I had powerful friends like Hoppy and Topper, whacked me with a pink hairbrush if I squirmed when she was trying to braid my hair. I was pretty squirmy. I wanted my mother to come back.

In those days, children, being considered noisy little germ factories, were not allowed in hospitals to visit. After several months, my father smuggled me in through the window in my mother's room. She was lying in bed in traction, with a body cast. The room smelled strongly of rubbing alcohol. She was smiling at me. I got a little fit of shyness. I wasn't quite sure what to say after all that time. There was a novelty song we knew from the radio. It went "Ah, get out of here with a [*drum sound effect*] *boom, boom, boom,* and don't come back no more!" Peter, Suzy, and I would sing it all over the house, banging the drum part on any resonant surface handy. I stepped up to the bed, belted the song out at the top of my lungs, and pounded the *boom, boom, boom* on her cast.

My mother exploded in laughter. The ice was broken. She showed me the picture of a Mexican guy in a big hat with a big-toothed grin that my father had drawn for her on her cast. She showed me the circle they had cut out of the front of her cast with a little electric saw, so she might be a bit cooler in that hot room in the middle of the desert before air-conditioning was in general use. The traction rig looked kind of fun, like a jungle gym for people who had to stay in bed. I didn't know she had been paralyzed. I didn't know that she had gone through a horrific surgery to try to make her walk again, incorporating a brand-new technique that might not even work. This involved taking a piece of her shin bone and grinding it up to make new pieces for her poor broken back, which was reassembled like a jigsaw puzzle and fused in place. During the six months my mother was in the hospital, that was the only time I got to see her.

When she finally came home, she was in bed for another six months, except she could take little steps with a walker. I played on the floor of her room all day, and we would listen to Rosemary Clooney and Bing Crosby sing live on the radio. I was ecstatic. I had my mother back.

In the second six months of her recovery, my mother began to make steady progress. She still had to wear a cast on her torso but gradually was able to do without the walker. She began to spend long hours with her sewing machine, making dresses that would fit over her cast and also pretty little cotton dresses for me and my sister to wear to school.

During the time that my mother was absent, I was used to a lot of freedom, roaming the desert with Dana on our ponies. So the idea of spending the day squirming in my desk in a stuffy classroom was not too popular with me. Peter and Suzy and all the O'Sullivan kids attended Saints Peter and Paul, the local Catholic school, and that was where I would be going in the fall. I had heard a lot of their stories and complaints. I was pretty excited about the brand-new pair of saddle shoes Mother bought for me, with plenty of room for my toes, but I would have traded them in a minute for the mud huaraches and more days to spend with Murphy.

I had always been extremely shy around other children. Before Dana, the only times I encountered other children were at my cousin Nina's birthday parties. I would be dressed up in pastel organdy and driven to my uncle's beautiful cattle ranch, the Agua Linda, which sprawled in the valley between Tucson and the Mexican border. Nina's mother would set a pretty table and have a wonderful lunch for us, including a cake that revolved on a music box stand. Then, after a hayride around my uncle's cotton fields, we would play pin the tail on the donkey and break a piñata. The other children would be scrambling for the candy, and I would peek out at them from behind my mother's leg, much too shy to participate.

At school, I knew I was going to have to contend with miserable shyness and no hayride.

As a little girl, I was taught that cowgirls don't cry. I didn't feel like a cowgirl the first day of school. I managed a few brave smiles for my father's camera but started to cry as soon as it was time to get in the car. My father took my hand and walked me, still crying, into my classroom. He thoughtfully introduced me to the sweet-faced little girl sitting across the aisle. Her name was Patsy, and she would become a lifelong and dearly loved friend, now godmother to my children and I to hers. I cried all day every day for three weeks. Then I finally gave up and just looked out the window.

The classroom that Patsy and I occupied was brand-new cinder block construction with a bank of windows on the left side and a cloakroom stretching along the entire back of the room.

We would file in there in the morning and stretch to put our lunch boxes on the shelf that ran above the row of hooks where we hung our coats. That was our one place to whisper and visit, because once we were seated in the classroom, we were expected to sit still with our hands folded on our desks and give our full attention to the front of the room. This was not always easy for such young children, especially some of the boys, and anyone who disobeyed was dealt with swiftly. I remember one unfortunate little boy who had wet his pants. The nun went after him, there was a struggle, and his desk tipped over onto the floor. She picked him up by his shirt collar, shook him loose from his desk, and then pulled him bawling back to the cloakroom and hung him on one of the available hooks by his belt. He was left there for a minute or two, utterly humiliated, flailing his little arms and legs furiously. This was shocking behavior to me. My parents never treated us like this—not even the thin-lipped Scottish woman did. If my mother had known that such things were going on in the classroom, she would have rammed Frank & Earnest through the convent wall. But we didn't tell her. We just said that we didn't like school. We thought this behavior was standard procedure at all schools, as we had never been to any other. I left for school each morning with a stomachache.

The class size was big—there were forty-eight of us—so the young nun standing in the front of the room might have envisioned Lilliputian anarchy if her crowd control methods were ineffective. She was dressed, poor thing, in a habit that consisted of a long-sleeved, ankle-length black wool dress, with heavy black stockings and lace-up black leather shoes. An elbow-length cape made of the same wool went over the pleated bodice and was never removed, even on the most blisteringly hot days. On her head was a black wool bonnet with a stiffly starched lining of white linen. The bonnet fastened snugly beneath her chin with a black bow. The starchy bit looked like it must surely scratch, and the tender skin at the side of her face was often streaked with red. At her waist was a long rosary with a heavy crucifix, the rustling sound of her rosary beads being synonymous with her movement. We learned to fear that sound because it could mean that she was coming up from behind to whack an offender with a ruler or, worse yet, the pointer.

To be made to dress in such a way in the desert heat was nothing short of sadistic. It made it very hard for the sisters to observe us properly on the playground, let alone play with us, as a minute spent in the full sun would turn the black habit into a solar collector that could incinerate its wearer. It's a wonder that the playground didn't turn into *Lord of the Flies*.

In the front of every classroom, above the blackboards, was a fairly large crucifix, fully loaded with a suffering Jesus and complement of thorny crown, nails, and oozing side gash. Whoever had the idea to force six-year-olds to contemplate an image of a man being horribly tortured to death was a sick person indeed. I thought the whole thing was gross and tried not to look. We were instructed that our childish peccadilloes had been responsible for this guy Jesus being treated in such a cruel fashion. Furthermore, they told us, he had eventually died to atone for what we did. I knew this couldn't possibly be true, because when all this stuff happened to him, I wasn't even born. This made me question the veracity of everything they ever told us.

An incident that stands out as a turning point in my ability to swallow any life-defining ideas not accompanied by data and published in a peer-reviewed journal occurred when I was in the second grade. Our teacher was Sister Francis Mary, a wizened old soul who had taught my father and Peter and Suzy before me. We actually liked her pretty well and tried hard to please her. She had established a point system to gauge our good behavior. This is how it worked: Sister Francis Mary hung a piece of paper on the wall. Sometimes she would leave the room for a short while, and if we were completely quiet and sitting with our hands folded when she returned, she would stick a gummed foil star on the paper. If we got ten stars, that meant we got to have a party.

In our class, we had a sweet girl, Bojanna, with thick, beautiful hair to her waist, whose family was Polish. Her mother made a traditional sweet called a Polish rosette, which was made out of fried dough and sprinkled with powdered sugar. When we had a party, Bojanna's mother would fry up fifty of them and bring them to school for the party. They were the most delicious things we ever tasted, and we really wanted to earn those ten stars and have our party.

One May afternoon, after we had earned almost enough stars and were in the home stretch for the party, Sister Francis Mary left the room. We had set up the traditional May altar in the corner, with a large plaster statue of the Virgin Mary and some flat pieces of scenery made to look like trees in a garden. Each morning, a different child would be responsible for bringing in a little wreath made of fresh flowers. We would all sing a song to the Virgin Mary, she would be crowned with the wreath, and it was a big deal. That particular afternoon after Sister left, we were being good, and we were being quiet. Patsy was walking up and down the aisles with her finger pressed to her lips as an extra reminder, and we were all thinking of the party and the Polish rosettes. The windows at the side of the classroom had been left open because it was a warm day, and a wind had kicked up. This can happen very suddenly in the desert, and the wind can be quite violent. The wind surged through the open windows and blew down a piece of scenery, which crashed into the Virgin Mary, knocking her to the floor and snapping her head off at the neck. The head rolled across the floor in front of our horrified gazes and came to a stop at about the third row. We couldn't have been more shocked if Marie Antoinette herself had been executed before us with a guillotine.

We were speechless and frozen in place when Sister Francis Mary returned. She was apoplectic. She demanded to know who had been roughhousing. Brave Patsy raised her hand and told Sister Francis Mary about the wind. Sister accepted her explanation. Then she wheeled on us and hissed that we in the class must have been having impure and sinful thoughts, that we were clearly wicked children, and that she was canceling all the stars we had earned. We were devastated. We hadn't been thinking impure thoughts. We had been thinking about the Polish rosettes.

I don't remember when there wasn't music going on in our house: my father whistling while he was figuring out how to fix something; my brother Pete practicing the "Ave Maria" for his performance with the Tucson Arizona Boys Chorus; my sister, Suzy, sobbing a Hank Williams song with her hands in the dishwater; my little brother, Mike, struggling to play the huge double bass.

Sundays, my father would sit at the piano and play most

anything in the key of C. He sang love songs in Spanish for my mother, and then a few Sinatra songs while he remembered single life before children, and responsibilities, and the awful war. My sister sang the role of Little Buttercup in a school production of *H.M.S. Pinafore* when she was in the eighth grade, so she and my mother would play from the big Gilbert and Sullivan book that sat on the piano. If they were in a frisky mood, they would sing "Strike Up the Band" or "The Oceana Roll." We would all harmonize with our mother on "Ragtime Cowboy Joe."

When we got tired of listening to our own house, we would tramp across the few hundred yards to the house of our Ronstadt grandparents, where we got a pretty regular diet of classical music. They had what they called a Victrola and would listen to their favorite opera excerpts played on 78 rpm recordings. *La Traviata*, *La Bohème*, and *Madama Butterfly* were the great favorites. On Saturdays they would tune in to the Metropolitan Opera radio broadcast or sit at the piano trying to unravel a simple Beethoven, Brahms, or Liszt composition from a page of sheet music.

Evenings, if the weather wasn't too hot or freezing, or the mosquitoes weren't threatening to carry us away to the Land of Oz, we would haul our guitars outside and sing until it was time to go in, which was when we had run out of songs.

There was no TV, the radio couldn't wander around with you because it was tethered to the wall, and we didn't get enough allowance to buy concert tickets. In any case, there weren't many big acts playing in Tucson, so if we wanted music, we had to make our own. The music I heard in those two houses before I was ten provided me with material to explore for my entire career.

Our parents sang to us from the time we were babies, and one haunting lullaby was often included in our nighttime ritual. It was a traditional song from northern Mexico that my father had learned from his mother, and it went like this:

Arriba en el cielo	Up in the sky
Se vive un coyote	There lives a coyote
Con ojos de plata	With silver eyes
Y los pies de azogue	And feet of mercury
Mátalo,	Kill it,
Mátalo por ladrón	Kill it for a thief
Lulo, que lulo	Lulo, Lulo
Que San Camaleón	Saint Camaleón
Debajo del suelo	From underneath the floor
Que salió un ratón	There goes a rat
Mátalo,	Kill it,
Mátalo, con un jalón	Kill it with a stake

Our mother had brought her own traditions from Michigan, and her songs were even grimmer. She sang us a song about Johnny Rebeck, whose wife accidentally ground him up in a sausage machine of his own invention. After that, she sang:

> Last night my darling baby died
> She died committing suicide
> Some say she died to spite us
> Of spinal meningitis
> She was a nasty baby anyway

We would howl with laughter and chorus back at her in three-part harmony:

> Oh, don't go in the cage tonight, Mother darling
> For the lions are ferocious and may bite
> And when they get their angry fits

They will tear you all to bits
So don't go in the lion's cage tonight

My favorite place for music was a *pachanga*. This was a Mexican rancher's most cherished form of entertainment. It was a picnic that took up an entire afternoon and evening and could last until midnight. Preparations would begin in the late afternoon, to avoid the worst heat of the day. A good site was chosen under a grove of cottonwood trees so there would be cool shade and a nice breeze. Someone would build a mesquite fire and grill steaks or pork ribs or whatever the local ranches provided. There would be huge, paper-thin Sonoran wheat tortillas being made by hand and baked on a *comal*, which is a smooth, flat piece of iron laid over the fire. Fragrant coffee beans were roasted over the fire too, then brewed and served with refried beans, white ranch cheese, homemade tamales, roasted corn, nopalitos, *calabasitas*, and a variety of chiles.

Around sunset, someone would uncork a bottle of tequila or the local *bacanora,* and people would start tuning up the guitars. The stars blinked on, and the songs sailed into the night. Mostly in Spanish, they were yearning, beautiful songs of love and desperation and despair. My father would often sing the lead, and then aunts, uncles, cousins, and friends joined in with whatever words they knew or whatever harmonies they could invent. The music never felt like a performance, it simply ebbed and flowed with the rest of the conversation. We children weren't sent off to bed but would crawl into someone's lap and fall asleep to the comforting sound of family voices singing and murmuring in two languages.

My brother Peter's beautiful boy soprano voice landed him a soloist's position in the Tucson Arizona Boys Chorus, which at the time had a national reputation. They would travel by private bus giving concerts throughout the country and return covered in aw-shucks glory. On the nights of their homecoming concerts, my father, mother, sister, and I would troop down to the Temple of Music and Art—a beautiful, small theater in downtown Tucson, modeled after the Pasadena Playhouse—and watch them sing. Our whole family would hold its collective breath while my brother emitted the eerie and mysterious high sounds that only prepubescent boy sopranos can make, praying that he wouldn't be sharp or flat. He was seldom either, but when he strayed, he was more likely to be sharp. I have the identical tendency. We all knew from hearing him practice at home which passages were likely to derail him, and we white-knuckled through them as we listened.

The boys were dressed in cowboy hats, silk neckerchiefs, satin-fringed and pearl-snapped cowboy shirts in desert sunset colors (the colors being allotted to sopranos and altos accordingly), bell-bottomed "frontier pants" with rodeo belt buckles, and cowboy boots. The stage was dressed with an artificial campfire, a starry-night backdrop, some saguaro cactus silhouettes, and a beautiful full moon projected from the back of the hall. Now, this was some serious production value, in my six-year-old opinion! It had a mesmerizing effect on the audience, and everyone listened in hushed and rapturous delight.

Whenever I imagined myself singing for the public, it would be like that: I would stand on a proscenium stage with a real curtain that opened and closed, and sing those beautiful, high, pure notes and give the audience chills. After all, I was a soprano too and could sing just as high as my brother. I wanted to sing like him. I can remember sitting at the piano. My sister was playing and my brother was singing something and I said, "I want to try that." My sister turned to my brother and said, "Think we got a soprano here." I was about four. I remember thinking, "I'm a singer, that's what I do." It was like I had become validated somehow, my existence affirmed. I was so pleased to know that that was what I was in life: I was a soprano. The idea of being famous or a star would not have been in my consciousness. I just wanted to sing and be able to make the sounds I had heard that had thrilled me so. And then one day, when I was fourteen, my sister and brother were singing a folk song called "The Columbus Stockade Blues." I came walking around the corner and threw in the high harmony. I did it in my chest voice and I surprised myself. Before that, I had tried to sing only in a high falsetto tone, and it didn't have any power.

Because my brother's voice was high and his performances were so central to our early family life, his sound was the first I ever tried to copy. All artists copy. We try as hard as we can to sound just like someone we admire; someone who evokes a strong feeling that we would like to emulate. The best part is, no matter how hard we try to copy, we wind up sounding like a version of ourselves.

The elements of voice and style are braided together like twine, consisting of these attempts to copy other artists, or an instrument, or even the sound of a bird or passing train. Added to these characteristics are emotions and thoughts that register as various vocal quirks, like hiccups, sighs, growls, warbles—a practically limitless assortment of choices. Most of these choices are made at the speed of sound on a subconscious level, or one would be completely overwhelmed by the task.

When I bend my ear to a singer's performance, I often try to track who it was that influenced him or her. For instance, I can hear Nat "King" Cole in early Ray Charles, Lefty Frizzell in early Merle Haggard, Rosa Ponselle in Maria Callas, Fats Domino in Randy Newman. In a recent duet with Tony Bennett, the late Amy Winehouse was channeling Dinah Washington and Billie Holiday to great effect, yet she still sounded like Amy Winehouse.

The regional accent one speaks also affects rhythms and phrasing, so someone who is "copying" has to import the accent too. For me, it helps to know the vocal bloodlines in order to decode the phrasing of a song. I once sang a Tom Petty song called "The Waiting," which has an intricate rhythm scheme for fitting lyrics into the music. Petty, an artist I admire, came along later than many classic rockers and so was able to absorb their elements into his writing and singing style. As I studied his vocal performance, it broke down something like this: Tom with his Florida accent was copying Mick Jagger with his British accent, who was copying Robert Johnson from the Mississippi Delta. And in another part of the same song, Tom was copying Roger McGuinn, who was copying Bob Dylan, who copied Woody Guthrie, who was in turn copying someone lost to our generation. These influences can show up in a whole line or just a word, or even the way that part of a word is attacked. As voices age, the vocal twine can become unraveled, and one hears the seams and joins of the laminated sound that has come to be recognized as that artist's style. It can collapse into a heap of ticks and quirks.

As kids growing up in the fifties, we tried to copy anything that inspired us from the radio, both in Spanish and English. We would harmonize on Hank Williams songs, Everly Brothers songs, or soap jingles. My father brought home a lot of records from Mexico. Of these, our favorites were the mysterious *huapangos*, sung by the Trio Calaveras and Trio Tariacuri. These songs from the mountains deep in Mexico had strange indigenous rhythms and vocal lines that broke into a thrilling falsetto. We also loved the urban smoothness of the jazz-based Trio Los Panchos.

I spent hours listening to the great ranchera singer Lola Beltrán. She influenced my singing style more than anyone. "Lola the Great" stood for Mexico as Edith Piaf stood for France. She had an enormous, richly colored voice that was loaded with drama, intrigue, and bitter sorrow. Although she was a belter who sang Mexican country music, her voice had the same dramatic and emotional elements as the opera singer Maria Callas. I listened to Callas with my grandmother. I read later in a Callas biography that she loved to sing along to the Mexican radio stations during trips she made to appear at the Dallas Opera. Lola was the most played female singer on Mexican radio. I am sure Callas loved her too.

When commercial folk music began to play on the radio in my early teens, we really paid attention. Here was something that sounded much like the Mexican traditional music on which we had been raised. Like the rancheras and huapangos, it was drawn from an earlier, agrarian life, was accompanied by acoustic instruments, and had rich, natural-sounding harmonies.

Peter, Suzy, and I hovered over recordings by popular folk trio Peter, Paul and Mary, and Canadian duo Ian and Sylvia. We would learn their songs and harmonies and then rearrange them for our own configuration of voices. I would cover the soprano-alto registers, Suzy the alto-tenor, and Pete would sing tenor-baritone. Years later, my younger brother, Mike, would sing whatever extra part was needed, from bass to high tenor. But he was still little then, so we formed a trio and called ourselves the New Union Ramblers. At the time, Suzy worked at the Union Bank, and I had an Arhoolie recording of the Hackberry Ramblers and thought *ramblers* sounded folky. We tried our best not to sound too treacly but were not always successful. We were having a lot of fun and sometimes played at the local folk clubs.

Bobby Kimmel, soon to become my Stone Poneys bandmate, played bass. He was short, with the dark, bearded look of the Beat Generation, and prone to quoting lengthy selections from his philosophy heroes, who ranged from the Indian writer Jiddu Krishnamurti to Lord Buckley, the hipster comic of the 1940s and 1950s.

Richard Saltus, a preppy, unusually tall and skinny schoolmate of mine, leaned over us playing the banjo and cracking us up with his quirky humor. He was unusually bright, years later becoming a science writer for the *Boston Globe*. He introduced me to Bill Monroe, the Stanley Brothers, Flatt and Scruggs, and the Blue Sky Boys. Again, their mountain harmonies reminded me of the Mexican trios and the huapangos I loved. They dealt with the same issues: the grueling work of living off the land and the treachery of misplaced affection.

My brother Pete went to work for the Tucson Police Department while he took his master's degree in government at the University of Arizona. He eventually became the chief of police, but at the time, the department didn't think too highly of my brother hanging around beatnik folk music clubs. My sister had three children and less time for music, so I began to play small venues on my own, sometimes with my cousin Bill Ronstadt accompanying me on the guitar. Bill, the most accomplished guitar player in our family, was a serious student of Brazilian music, but when he played with me, we did simpler American folk songs. The professional demands were not great. I could play a set of four or five songs, and Bill would fill in with Brazilian pieces. We occasionally got paid but felt lucky to get the experience of being in front of an audience. Sometimes Bobby Kimmel would play a set of blues tunes that he had worked out, and I would duet with him on a folkier piece like "Handsome Molly."

We played at a coffeehouse called Ash Alley and another

called the First Step. They were tiny, seventy- to one-hundred-seat places owned by local folk music entrepreneur David Graham.

His younger brother, Alan Fudge, sang and played guitar and was studying acting at the university. He was smart, funny, kind, and political. Alan and I spent most of our spare time at his brother's establishment and became sweethearts. His mother, Margaret, was the first feminist I ever encountered and would scold her sons robustly if they were careless with their girlfriends. She was divorced, and when her son David brought in older bluesmen like Sonny Terry and Brownie McGhee to play at his club, she would cook for them, let them stay at her house, and do what she could to cushion them from the bruising elements of Jim Crow still hovering in the Southwest. This was before the Civil Rights Act of 1964, and there were signs everywhere bragging about a proprietor's right to refuse service.

Conversations at their house were often about the hoped-for civil rights legislation, the Vietnam War (which few Americans were aware of at the time), and the unconscionable shenanigans of the House Un-American Activities Committee. At the public high school that I attended, my civics teacher, a Ukrainian, showed us films on the HUAC and warned us about the Communist threat that lurked behind every cactus. I also had an English teacher from the Deep South who spent one entire class period making an impassioned defense of the KKK, and awarded an A to anyone who read *Gone With the Wind*. At Margaret's house, I got another side of the story. She was not like any of the Tucson mothers I had ever met. A free spirit who insisted on personal responsibility, she was very kind to me.

Alan taught me songs he had learned from Pete Seeger and the Weavers about the labor movement. He was performing the lead in a university production of Shakespeare's *Othello*, and we explored that play together. One night he came home with two records: *Frank Sinatra Sings for Only the Lonely* and the first Bob Dylan album. I thought the Nelson Riddle arrangements on the Sinatra record were stunning. It was the first time I had ever heard Bob Dylan sing, and I liked that too. We spent many evenings dissecting those records. Some of my music friends thought those artists were diametrically opposed, one from "the establishment" and the other from the foment of cultural revolution. I thought they were both great storytellers.

In those days, Top Forty radio was still regional and had a wide-open playlist. When I drove to school, I could turn on the radio and hear George Jones, Dave Brubeck, the Beach Boys, and the Singing Nun on the same station. I much prefer that style of radio to the corporate model we have today, with tightly formatted playlists and the total absence of regional input.

Alan's brother continued to try to build a following for folk music at the First Step. He brought in ace bluegrass band the Kentucky Colonels with Clarence White and his brother Roland. I would watch Clarence night after night, his face an expressionless mask while he flat-picked notes at speeds not equaled until the invention of the particle accelerator.

David also brought Kathy and Carol, a duo who sang Elizabethan ballads and Carter Family songs. They were good guitar players, especially Carol, and their complex, shimmering harmonies were completely original. The two were both natural beauties, innocent and full of wonder. Still teenagers, they had an Elektra Records recording contract, were playing folk festivals around the country, and getting to hear and jam with major folk artists that I had read about in *Sing Out!* magazine.

I remember seeing blues singer Barbara Dane and guitarist Dick Rosmini at David's club. Dick complimented my voice and encouraged me to go to Los Angeles and see what was happening at the Ash Grove, an L.A. coffeehouse that played traditional music to enthusiastic crowds. Tucson being a relatively small city, the folk music venues always struggled, and the shows were poorly attended. I began to wish I could go someplace that had a richer, more diverse, and more appreciated pool of music.

Alan left Tucson to play Shakespeare at the Old Globe Theatre in San Diego. Bobby had gone east to Massachusetts to spend time with friends in the Jim Kweskin Jug Band. He wrote to me about this girl singer they had added named Maria D'Amato, who was gorgeous and could really sing. She married his friend Geoff Muldaur, the other star singer in the Kweskin band, and became Maria Muldaur. Geoff was a great admirer of blues singer Sleepy John Estes and cobbled together his own compelling and original style from that influence. Geoff in turn had a strong influence on the singing style of John Sebastian, later a founding member of the Lovin' Spoonful. After spending some time on Martha's Vineyard with the Kweskin band, Kimmel went to the West Coast and moved in with Malcolm Terence, a friend from Tucson who was a reporter for the *Los Angeles Times*.

My mother and I drove to the coast the summer of 1964 to visit my aunt Luisa, then resident hostess at the Southwest Museum of the American Indian in Los Angeles. Knowing I wanted to sing, Aunt Luisa had sent me a recording, *Duets with the Spanish Guitar*, which featured guitarist Laurindo Almeida dueting alternately with flautist Martin Ruderman and soprano Salli Terri. It became one of my most cherished recordings.

She and Terri were close friends, and when I told her how much I loved the record, she invited me to meet her. My aunt had helped her research material for her recordings, plus she coached her pronunciation when she sang in Spanish. Aunt

Luisa also gave Terri many of the costumes she had worn during the course of her own career. They now belong to the Southwest Museum. She drove us to Olvera Street, the original center of Los Angeles, and showed us the theater where she herself had sung while wearing those beautiful costumes, sometime during the 1920s.

Alan drove up from San Diego, and he and I spent the evening with Bobby at Malcolm's little place at the beach. Bobby was playing in small clubs and said that if I wanted to come over, he could find us work. There weren't many opportunities left for me in Tucson. David hadn't been able to succeed with the First Step and had to close it. I decided to think about it. I was eighteen and enrolled for the spring semester at the University of Arizona in Tucson.

I made plans to drive to the coast and visit Bobby again during spring break of 1965. I traveled with some friends who were going to get summer jobs in canneries in California and return to school in the fall. We all slept on the sofa or the floor or anywhere we could fit.

Bobby was eager to introduce me to a guitar player he had met named Kenny Edwards. He worked at McCabe's Guitar Shop, which was in the front lobby of the Ash Grove, a club on Melrose, then the mecca for West Coast folkies. We jammed all of us into somebody's car and drove to West Hollywood. We found Kenny seated with a guitar, playing a flashy finger-picked version of "Roll Out the Barrel." It was a nightly ritual that he engaged in with another guitarist who worked there. They would try to outplay each other and also show off the guitars they had for sale. Kenny was tall, with the athletic body of a surfer. He was skeptical and intellectual, dark featured and handsome. He dressed like a disheveled English schoolboy, and at nineteen, his guitar playing was impressive. He suggested we move from the lobby into the performing space of the Ash Grove to hear a new band call the Rising Sons. Kenny loved their two guitar players, Taj Mahal and Ry Cooder. Though just young kids, they played like demons, with confidence and skill far beyond their years. They were dead serious about the music.

Driving back to the beach, Malcolm and Bobby started talking about a new L.A. band called the Byrds, who were playing folk rock, a new hybrid taking hold on the West Coast. Eventually, we went to see them at the Trip, a new club on the Sunset Strip that had a light show and was supposed to give you a psychedelic experience with your music. As soon as I heard their creamy harmonies, I was mesmerized. I recognized Chris Hillman from a bluegrass band I'd heard, the Scottsville Squirrel Barkers. In that band, he had played mandolin. Now he was playing bass guitar in an electric band with Beatle haircuts. It was clear to me that music was happening on a whole different level in Los Angeles. I began making plans to move to L.A. at the end of the spring semester.

I turned in my final exam to my English professor, the noted Arizona poet Richard Shelton. He was also an autoharp player and sometimes joined us at family jam sessions. The final was an essay on something from Yeats that he had written on the blackboard. He said he hoped he would see me in the fall. I told him I was moving to Los Angeles to sing in a folk-rock band. Justifiably bemused, he replied, "Well, Miss Ronstadt, I wish you luck."

I still hadn't told my parents. I knew they would insist that I was too young, hadn't finished school, and had no real way to support myself. I also knew they were right, but I had to go where the music was.

I waited until the night I left to tell them. A musician friend had offered me a ride to the coast. He had gigs north of L.A. and offered to drop me off on the way. My parents were upset and tried to talk me out of it. When it became apparent that they couldn't change my mind, my father went into the other room and returned with the Martin acoustic guitar that his father had bought brand new in 1898. When my father began singing as a young man, my grandfather had given him the instrument and said, *"Ahora que tienes guitarra, nunca tendrás hambre"* ("Now that you own a guitar, you will never be hungry"). My father handed me the guitar with the same words. Then he took out his wallet and gave me thirty dollars. I made it last a month.

The only thing I remember about that long ride through the desert night was searing remorse for having defied my parents. I was still very attached, and they had always been so kind to me. I felt terrible for hurting them and causing them worry. There was nothing to be done. My new life was beginning to take shape.

On the front steps of a Hart Street bungalow. I am wearing the
denim divided skirt that my mother bought in the 1930s so she could ride
a horse "Western style."

2

Hart Street

THE HOUSE WHERE I lived with Bobby and Malcolm was a little clapboard bungalow in Ocean Park, the neighborhood between the Santa Monica and Venice Piers. The Santa Monica Pier had an early-twentieth-century wooden carousel with beautiful hand-carved fantasy horses. Lacking the flesh-and-blood variety, I would ride the wooden ones and dream. There was only a parking lot between our house and the broad sands of Santa Monica Beach. The area was filled with ramshackle Victorian beach cottages, and the rents were cheap. Some interesting people lived in the area, most notably Charles Seeger, the eminent musicologist (and father of Pete Seeger), who lived directly across the street. He can be seen in the neighborhood crowd picture that we used on the back cover of the third Stone Poneys album, along with singer-songwriter Tim Buckley, who lived around the corner. Our friend Ron Pearlman, a writer for the hit TV comedy *The Beverly Hillbillies*, lived at the other end of the block. He told me that his old college roommate was an agent who had worked his way up from a job in the mailroom at the William Morris Agency. He was moving to the West Coast and was interested in getting into the music business. Ron said he was an unusually bright guy and very charming. He was eager to introduce us. His name was David Geffen.

We settled into a nice domestic routine on Hart Street. Malcolm was a serious cook and laid out a feast for the entire household on a nightly basis. He made everything from complicated Indian dishes to matzo brei. On Sundays we baked bread. While the dough was rising, we would walk down the beach to the sea-food market on the Santa Monica Pier and buy fresh clams to steam for breakfast. I cleaned. The rest of the time Bobby, Kenny, and I rehearsed until we had enough songs to play a show. Our school friends from Tucson would come stay for a few days on their way to their summer jobs, sleep on whatever bit of floor space they could claim, and we would sing our new stuff for them. The house was full, and there was always an interesting conversation.

The Troubadour is a nightclub in West Hollywood, about twenty minutes from where we lived in Santa Monica. Like the Ash Grove, it featured a lot of acoustic acts but also included some mainstream music and comedy. It had an open-mike night on Mondays, called Hoot Night, which also served as a way to audition. Playing there under any circumstance guaranteed you exposure to people in the music business. It was well attended by record company executives, managers, and agents. Other performers also hung out in the bar and kept an eye on new de-velopments in the burgeoning L.A. music scene. Bobby, Kenny, and I, calling ourselves the Stone Poneys after a Charlie Patton blues song, played a Hoot Night and were hired to open for Odetta, one of my folk music heroes. We were politely received by Odetta's audience. It was our first time to perform in such a high-profile place, and we were excited just to have the chance.

Soon after that, a man came up to me in the Troubadour bar. I recognized him as the owner of a restaurant nearby. It was a wonderful place to eat, but we could rarely afford it. He asked me to come to his restaurant the next afternoon. He wanted to talk business. I assumed that he might be interested in helping us buy some equipment or getting us a record deal. The next day, I took the bus from the beach up Wilshire Boulevard and walked the few blocks from the bus stop to the restaurant.

Considerably older than I, he was still handsome, European,

and had rather formal manners. I sat across the table from him in the empty restaurant, and he got right to the point. He told me that I was still very young, didn't seem to have a dependable source of income, was likely to be facing some difficult times ahead, and he could make life much easier for me. He would pay for a nice apartment, buy my clothes, and give me a generous allowance of spending money. In return, I would be expected to sleep with him. I was dumbfounded. I stammered that I couldn't imagine sleeping with someone for any reason other than love. Furthermore, I thought I was doing well. I was getting paid for singing and lived with Malcolm and Bobby in our cool hippie crash pad at the beach. My mother was still making my clothes for me on her sewing machine. He remained perfectly polite as he accepted my refusal, and we concluded our conversation.

I returned to Santa Monica on the bus. I hardly knew what to say to Kenny and Bobby, who were back at Hart Street waiting to see if we were going to get some new amps. When I told them what had happened, they were as astonished as I was. In the era of free love, no one we knew thought about paying for sex. He was from another generation.

Another man approached me at the Troubadour the night we auditioned. His name was Herb Cohen. We had just come down from the stage, when he appeared at my side and said he wanted to talk. A British comedian that I knew leaned between us and said to me, "Linda, this is an important man. Listen to what he says." Herb took a firm hold on my elbow and guided me out through the Troubadour bar to a restaurant next door. Bobby and Ken were following behind.

Herb wasn't one to mince words. He looked straight at Kimmel and said, "I can get your girl singer a record deal. I don't know about the band." I was distressed by this remark. I felt I owed them my loyalty. I wasn't ready to be a solo act, and I knew it. We didn't know much about Herb, either. He said he could try for a deal that included the band but no guarantees. We told him we needed some time to talk about it. People told us that Herb had a reputation for being a tough guy.

Dick Rosmini, the guitarist I had met earlier in Tucson, was a well-established studio musician in Los Angeles. He also worked as a photographer and a commercial artist. He seemed to know a lot about the music scene there. Dick had turned up at our Troubadour shows to shoot pictures, and he continued to give advice and encouragement. We asked him what he knew about Herb. According to Dick, Herb was a complicated guy, but he liked him. Herb had strong political convictions. He had fought in Cuba on the side of Fidel Castro. After that, he was a soldier of fortune in Sudan. He then began to run guns for the Congolese rebels. He would take a load of Algerian hashish to Paris, sell it, and use the money to buy guns. Then he would smuggle the guns back into the Congo.

One afternoon he was in his hotel in Paris with the cash from the hashish sale, waiting to make a gun deal. His phone rang, and he picked it up. "Leave" was the only thing he heard from the voice at the other end. He looked out the window and saw the police coming in the front door. Herb threw the money in an empty suitcase and walked out the back door. At the airport, he bought a razor, shaved off his beard, and boarded a plane for the United States. He arrived at Rosmini's apartment with the suitcase full of money and a strong desire to find a safer line of work. Herb used the money from the gunrunning operation to open a Los Angeles folk music coffeehouse called the Unicorn. Lenny Bruce worked there regularly, and they were friends. Judy Henske worked there too, and he became her manager.

Judy was a striking brunette, really tall and really smart. She was a kind of chanteuse who sang blues and told incredibly funny stories onstage. She had a wicked tongue. I had met her in the Troubadour bar. I was newly arrived from Tucson, and she might have felt a surge of pity for me sitting there looking neither hip nor savvy. On the other hand, it could have been a surge of pure contempt. "Honey," she said at the top of her voice (Judy always talked at the top of her voice), "I am going to tell you something. In this town there are four sexes: men, women, homosexuals, and girl singers."

I decided to accept her remark in the spirit of solidarity. It was a valuable piece of information.

The allure of a record deal and some guidance from a manager finally outweighed Herb's exotic reputation, and we signed a management contract with him. I grew to like him very much. He had settled down with a pretty wife and a little daughter that he clearly adored.

By this time, he was handling Tim Buckley plus Frank Zappa and the Mothers of Invention. He and Zappa would later start a couple of record labels, Straight and Bizarre. He also booked what were called "Freak Out" dance performances for the GTOs, a quartet of girl groupies Zappa had assembled that included the legendary Miss Pamela (now Pamela Des Barres).

Miss Pamela, undoubtedly the model for the character Penny Lane in the Cameron Crowe film *Almost Famous*, was as beautiful as a fawn. She seemed guileless, with an underlying kindness and a keen sensitivity. Never cloying, her preternatural sweetness produced a head-spinning effect.

Zappa was also something of a patron to the infamous Cynthia Plaster Caster, renowned for having captured the plaster impressions of erect penises belonging to the various rock stars she admired. She also kept detailed accounts of the experiences in a journal.

The plaster penises were housed in a filing cabinet in the Bizarre Records offices. When someone wanted to see them, Pauline, the leggy, miniskirted British secretary, would pull out the file drawer. They would glide into view, trembling and shivering from the motion of the drawer, resplendent in their plastery tumescence. They gave the impression of a tiny forest, with Jimi Hendrix's unmistakably distinguished as the mightiest oak in the wood.

Unlike his reputation, Herb's household and office furnishings were tasteful and refined. In his travels, he had amassed a beautiful collection of antiques and Middle Eastern rugs. Everything he owned seemed to have an adventure behind it. Herb wasn't very tall, but he was powerfully built and had an aura of willful determination that few would think wise to oppose.

One night we were watching Tim Buckley at the Troubadour. Herb was standing at the door with a clicker that counted all the customers who came in. That way the club owner couldn't hold back on the artist's share of the gate. Someone started to heckle Tim. Herb pulled a ballpoint pen out of his pocket and shoved it into the guy's ribs, told him it was a gun, and pushed him out into the street. He came back inside laughing his cynical, infectious laugh. His strength lay in the fact that if he fooled other people, he never fooled himself.

He took us to the Capitol Records Tower in Hollywood, the famous "round" building that resembles a stack of 45 records on a record player spindle. We rode the elevator up to Nik Venet's office. Nik had agreed to produce us, and we were given a boilerplate recording contract to sign. Nik was a staff producer for Capitol and had made some records with the Beach Boys. He was fast talking and charming, more Las Vegas in his sensibility than the Ash Grove folkie world I thought I had left home to find.

Musically, our band was very green and hadn't gained much strength in the short time that we had been together. It showed in the recordings we made. After the release of our debut album in January of 1967, Capitol sent us on a promotional tour of the folk club circuit that existed in the United States in those days. The clubs were really important to the development of the music because they provided an entry-level atmosphere where the artists could learn and get experience with audiences across the country. They also gave us a chance to hear artists in other places and see how we compared. That was humbling. We played Detroit, Philadelphia, Boston, and New York. It was the first time I had ever been to the East Coast. We opened for the Paul Butterfield Blues Band at the Cafe Au Go-Go in New York's Greenwich Village. The air-conditioning was louder than we were.

In Boston, Bobby renewed his friendship with the Jim Kweskin Jug Band, and we spent some time getting to know them. An acoustic band, they reigned supreme at the Club 47 in Cambridge, near Harvard Square. People would jam the place to hear them play. Tall, skinny, ginger-haired Fritz Richmond played the bass lines either by blowing on a jug or by slapping a washtub rigged with one string and what looked like a broom handle. Using the handle for a lever, he could change the tension on the string to raise or lower the pitch. They also played fiddles, guitars, kazoos, and washboards with impressive musicianship. Men in the audience were simply drooling over Maria, who had the curves and nonplussed sexuality of Betty Boop. Her intelligent phrasing and sincere charm guaranteed that she would not be dismissed on any level.

I remember having a conversation in the Troubadour bar with Janis Joplin, who also loved Maria's singing. She had been telling me with touching excitement about how the new dress she was wearing made her feel pretty, and she had come to the Troubadour to show it off. We got into a discussion about what we liked to wear onstage and immediately agreed that Maria was the gold standard of glamour for the hippie/earthy segment of our society. Because of the phenomenal success of artists like the Rolling Stones and Bob Dylan, earthy funk was God, and the female performers in the folk pop genre were genuinely confused about how to present themselves. Did we want to be nurturing, stay-at-home earth mothers who cooked and nursed babies, or did we want to be funky mamas in the Troubadour bar, our boot heels to be wandering an independent course just like our male counterparts? We didn't know. Later, I did my own exasperated send-up of our confusion by posing for an album cover in a pen with pigs in the style of the character Moonbeam McSwine from the comic strip *Li'l Abner* that I had read in the *Tucson Daily Citizen*.

Our first record didn't sell, and we began to discuss material for a second attempt. I felt that the songs Bobby was writing for us weren't good vehicles for my voice. Ken and Bobby had a conflicting vision of the band's musical direction. I began to look around for outside material. I found a song called "Different Drum" on a bluegrass record sung by John Herald of the Greenbriar Boys and written by Mike Nesmith before he joined the Monkees. I told Venet I thought it was a hit. We went into the studio and recorded an arrangement for acoustic instruments, with Kenny playing mandolin. Venet wasn't happy with it and said he wanted to hire an outside arranger, Jimmy Bond, and recut it. A few days later, I walked into the studio and was surprised to see it filled with musicians I had never met. They were all good players: Don Randi on harpsichord, Jimmy Gordon on the drums, and Bond playing bass. There was also an acoustic guitar and some strings. The arrangement was completely different from the way I had rehearsed it. I tried as hard as I could to sing it, but we went through it only twice, and I hadn't had time to learn the new arrangement. I told Venet I didn't think we could use it because it was so different from the way I had imagined it. Also, it didn't include Bobby or Ken. He ignored me. It was a hit.

The first time we heard the recording of "Different Drum" on the radio, we were on our way to Hollywood for a meeting with Nik Venet and Jimmy Bond to discuss material and arrangements for a third album. We were out of money. Our meager advances had already been used to pay rent and bills and repair Bobby's car, the only one we had among the three of us. It still wasn't running well. Somewhere in West L.A., something froze in the engine, and the car began its death cry—a hideous sound of metal straining against metal. We rode our screaming vehicle several blocks, turning heads in the street. When it finally refused to budge, we got out and pushed it into a gas station. The mechanic, who had heard us from blocks away, explained to us that the car, which was loaded with our guitars, Bobby's huge acoustic bass, and, recently, us, would never run again and could only be sold for scrap.

The jingle for KRLA, an L.A. Top Forty AM station, sounded weakly from the back of the station's garage. It was followed by the four measures of acoustic guitar–harpsichord introduction to "Different Drum," and then me singing. We strained to hear it. We knew that it was getting airplay in San Francisco but didn't know if it would make the national playlists. Hearing it on KRLA meant it had.

Someone eventually showed up to rescue us, and when we got to Nik's office and began to discuss our new recording, we realized being carless in L.A. wasn't our only problem. Capitol was adamant that the new record be titled *Linda Ronstadt, Stone Poneys and Friends, Vol. III.* They wanted me to step out firmly in front so that I could be identified as the lead singer. No boost to band morale, it was the beginning of the end for the Stone Poneys.

We had been performing as a harmony band featuring Kimmel's compositions and me as an occasional soloist. Now we had to assemble a repertoire that made me sound like a lead singer with material and a style we didn't have, and we had to do it fast. "Different Drum" was a national Top Forty hit. To expose us to larger audiences, Herb Cohen had gotten us some dates opening for the Doors, who had just had a huge hit with "Light My Fire."

In March 1968 we started the tour in Utica, a college town in upstate New York. As the opening act, we were well tolerated by the audience and the Doors members were nice to us. Ray Manzarek, John Densmore, and Robby Krieger were all excellent players who seemed to be solid guys. Their singer, Jim Morrison, was moody and distant, and I noticed that he liked to drink. I watched their show with a great deal of curiosity. The dynamic between the audience and the performers was different from what I had observed in the folkier musical environment that had been my previous experience. Some individuals in the audience seemed to be projecting themselves onto Morrison. This was followed by a kind of needy, narcissistic frenzy that seemed dangerous and unhealthy. Morrison would pick up the microphone stand like it was a javelin and posture with it, as though he needed to protect himself from the identity-bending onslaught of the crowd's adoration. I found it troubling.

Backstage after the show, some girls invited us to their apartment. Kenny went with us and some of the Doors, including Morrison. The girls were college students, earnest, young, and excited to have Morrison in their tidy little apartment. He had brought along a bottle that he emptied steadily, and after a while, he began knocking things over. The girls looked embarrassed, as if they weren't sure whether or not it was an accident. Kenny and I were sure it wasn't and hightailed it out of there immediately. In the morning, we heard that he had trashed their little place, and a hefty bill was presented for the damages.

The following day in nearby Rochester, Bob Neuwirth joined the tour. I believe the Doors' management sent him to be an auxiliary road manager to try to keep Morrison out of trouble. I had met Neuwirth through mutual friends in the Kweskin Jug Band, and he had also made an appearance in the Bob Dylan documentary *Don't Look Back* as Dylan's sidekick. Himself a capable musician and songwriter, he was smart, funny, and socially adept.

The next day we had a show in Boston. We went to the airport early in the morning to find that a massive snowstorm had grounded all the planes. Herb didn't want to lose money from a canceled show, so we waited several hours while he chartered a DC-3 passenger aircraft. But we still didn't have a pilot. After more time waiting around, Herb found someone who flew in his spare time — he worked for a used tire company — and was willing to take us there in spite of the weather. The turbulence was extreme. We were all green faced with motion sickness, and in a propeller plane, it took us two and a half hours to get to Boston. I had to dress in the tiny airplane lavatory. Mohawk Airlines had lost one of my suitcases on the way to Utica, and all I had was my wrinkled Betsey Johnson striped singing dress that I had stuffed into my purse. No shoes or tights. I ran across the snowy tarmac in bare feet and a lightweight coat, hopped into a waiting station wagon, and was driven directly to the 3,200-seat Back Bay Theater. When we walked onstage, we were greeted by the audience chanting "We want the Doors!" They were furious that they had been kept waiting, and their patience was exhausted. I sang "Different Drum" and beat it off the stage.

After Boston, we had a day off in New York before playing the Fillmore East, a newly opened 2,400-seat theater operated by soon-to-become-legendary rock concert promoter Bill

Graham. It was only the second show he had presented at that venue. Big Brother and the Holding Company had officially opened it the week before. During the wild ride in the DC-3 to Boston, Morrison and I had been chatting, and he asked if I wanted to spend some time with him on our free evening. Sober, he seemed sweet and somewhat shy. I knew that Bob Neuwirth would be going with us and figured he could keep him under control, so I agreed. Neuwirth suggested that we go to hear the Kweskin Jug Band, which was playing in New York.

My friend Liisa, a flaxen-haired, doll-faced beauty from Finland, had an apartment in Greenwich Village. We had been best friends in Tucson during our high school years.

In her teens, she was abruptly transplanted from Finland to the Arizona desert by her father, a physicist working at the university on the project to land a man on the moon. Her parents were divorced, so my mother took Liisa under her wing, and they spent hours sewing together. She and my mother sewed my favorite stage dress from a pattern that Liisa created. A talented designer, she had a job in New York and had decorated her tiny apartment beautifully. I liked to stay with her whenever I was in New York, and we would renew our cozy friendship.

Liisa's apartment was only a few blocks from the Cafe Au Go-Go, where the Jug Band was playing. Neuwirth and Morrison came to the apartment to get me, and Liisa declined our invitation to come along. We were walking along the street looking for a good place to have dinner when a man driving by recognized Morrison, slammed on his brakes, jumped out of the car, walked up to Morrison, and punched him in the face. I managed to get in between them, and Neuwirth ran the fellow off. We proceeded to dinner. Morrison ordered a drink to steady his nerves and a few more after that. By the time we got to the Cafe Au Go-Go, he was quite drunk.

Backstage before the show, Maria took me and Neuwirth

aside and confided that she was in low spirits because the band was breaking up. It would be one of their last shows together. Neuwirth and I were huge admirers of the Jug Band, and truly sad to hear it. We resolved to give her all the support we could from the audience. Morrison, clearly impressed by their musicianship and Maria's earthy glamour, wanted to join in our enthusiasm, but in his extreme condition, all he could do was to stand up and slur "You lil' fuckerz!" at the top of his voice. Neuwirth and I, mortified, decided to get him out of there so he wouldn't ruin the show.

We walked the few blocks back to Liisa's building. It was early still, and Morrison said he wanted to come back up and hang out. Thinking of Liisa's pristine jewel box of a home and remembering the fate of the girl's apartment on our first night, I slipped inside the building and closed the door firmly. I didn't want to be embarrassed in front of another friend. Morrison was pounding on the glass, ringing doorbells, and yelling that he wanted to come in. I smiled sweetly at him through the glass and pantomimed that I was sleepy, hoping to calm him down. He grew more belligerent. I ran up to Liisa's apartment and slid the security bolt in place. From the window, I could see him still yelling and Neuwirth pulling on his arm.

We went to sound check at the Fillmore East the next afternoon. Bill Graham was walking around barking orders and wearing a yellow hard hat. He explained that the last time the Doors played one of his events, Morrison hurled the heavy microphone stand into the audience, injuring some people. He had made it contractually clear to the Doors that if the incident was repeated, they wouldn't get paid, but he put on the hard hat just in case.

Morrison arrived eventually. He was accompanied by a beautiful girl with long red hair. She was bruised from her jaw to her collarbone. "Oh," she said, when someone asked what had happened to her. "I ran into a door."

3

Going Solo

Photo by Henry Diltz.

WE RETURNED TO LOS Angeles and an uncertain future. Kenny left the band and traveled to India. Bobby took a job running a concert series at McCabe's Guitar Shop, where we had first met Kenny. It was to be a deeply satisfying experience for him that lasted many years. Sometime later, Kenny joined my backup band, and we recorded and toured together for years. We all remained friends.

Kenny and Bobby were officially taken off the accounting books at Capitol Records, which meant that, as they were no longer members of the Stone Poneys, they weren't responsible for paying back the production costs of the three albums we had made together. However, they then began to share in the royalties accrued by the sales of "Different Drum." I assumed the debt burden by myself, and it would be eight years before I would see any money from record sales. Meanwhile, if I wanted to earn a living in music, I had to hit the road.

I was painfully unprepared to be a solo act, as I had been mostly a harmony singer in the Stone Poneys. We had relied on

Kimmel to write the songs, and I had no repertoire of my own. I began to think what I could use from the music I had loved as a child in Tucson. The obvious answer was to experiment with the 1950s country songs I had learned from my sister's collection of 45s and the jukeboxes in rural Arizona. They had simple chord progressions, so I started to work up songs like Ray Price's "Crazy Arms" and Hank Williams's "I Can't Help It (If I'm Still In Love With You)" on my guitar.

Herb thought I was wasting my time. He said I would be too country for the rock stations and too rock for the country stations. I ignored him and began to look for musicians who could play the songs that had come out of Nashville but with a California twist.

Clarence White, the poker-faced bluegrass flat-picker I so admired in Tucson, had joined the Byrds and was playing what he called his B-Bender guitar. With drummer Gene Parsons (no relation to Gram), he had designed and installed on his Fender Telecaster a device that raised the second string a whole step, making it sound like a pedal steel guitar. The lever that raised and lowered the string was attached to the guitar strap and activated by pushing down on the guitar neck. It became a cornerstone of the California country rock sound.

Other guitar players got wind of the device and began to incorporate it into their own styles. One of them was Bernie Leadon. Bernie, a musician who had played bluegrass, folk music, and rock and roll, had the most musically integrated overview of all the seminal country rock guitar players in the Troubadour pantheon. In his early twenties, he was already an outstanding player who had mastered a variety of styles. He was also a solid, reliable guy, more ambitious for the music to be good than he was to make himself noticed. Players like that are crucial to any emerging musical process and often make essential contributions that remain hidden because they lack the showboating gene. Like Clarence, Bernie became another pioneer of the country rock guitar style — one that exerted a powerful influence on all of popular music when he became a founding member of the Eagles.

I met him in the Stone Poneys days when he was in the psychedelic country folk band Hearts and Flowers. He and Larry Murray, also in the band, had been in the Scottsville Squirrel Barkers with Chris Hillman, before Chris joined the Byrds. Hearts and Flowers recorded on Capitol and Nik Venet hired Bernie and Larry to play on the Stone Poneys recordings. Larry left the band in 1969 to write for Johnny Cash's new music variety TV program, *The Johnny Cash Show,* and Bernie eventually joined the Flying Burrito Brothers with Chris and Gram Parsons. We all hung out at the Troubadour and began jamming together, united by our mutual desire to weld country music songs and harmonies to a rock-and-roll rhythm section.

Putting together a band for a style of music that hadn't yet coalesced was no easy task. Herb, who saw things in business terms only, had no musical ability and was unable to help me. His advice was to call the musicians' union, ask them to send over any guitar player, and tell him what to play. Of course, music is not made this way.

When I hire a musician to record or perform, the first thing I look for is a shared sensibility. Whatever the musician listened to or read or saw or where he lived growing up informs every note he plays in a myriad of ways. There are so many choices to make — how loud or soft to play a note, exactly where to place it rhythmically, what kind of textural or melodic embellishment to incorporate, where to add a harmony, how to voice a chord — all done in a split second. It simply can't be done on a conscious level but becomes a matter of instinct enabled by long practice. When a compatible group of players is assembled to serve a clearly defined musical vision, the result can be pure joy. If the group lacks a shared sensibility, it is pure misery.

Since I'd had a hit record, it was fairly easy for Herb to get me on television. I thought that TV, with its small screens and tinny speakers, was a bad medium for music. Also, artists had no say in how they were presented in those days, and one might be expected to wear a costume of the show's design that was color coordinated to its sets. The musical director also might burden the music with cumbersome orchestral arrangements not in the style or spirit of the artist or the original recordings.

In the spring of 1969, I went to Nashville to perform on *The Johnny Cash Show*. I had traveled with a fellow from Herb's office charged with getting me to Tennessee and making sure everything ran smoothly once we got there. He apparently had more important things to do and, after getting me settled at the hotel, flew on to Detroit.

I was a little worried about being left to fend for myself but soon connected with my Troubadour pal Larry Murray. He and the other writers for the show, plus production staff and guests, were being housed at the Ramada Inn, where I was staying. I wound up in Larry's room in a jam session with a few of the up-and-coming Nashville songwriters that Larry knew. Mickey Newberry and Kris Kristofferson were among them, and not yet well known. They had piles of good songs that no one had ever recorded.

Everybody played his best new stuff, and then we got into a conversation about culture shock and what it was like for Larry to be a long-haired hippie working in the South. Larry confessed that he often felt out of place and lonely, even threatened, and that he missed hanging out at the Troubadour, where he looked perfectly normal.

It was beginning to get late, so I went back to my room to get some sleep for the read-through and rehearsal the following morning. Immediately after I closed my door, the phone rang. It was one of the show's producers, whom I had met briefly earlier in the day. He wanted to come to my room and discuss some of the details of the show. Since I had no one from my management to help negotiate for me, and since he was essentially a stranger and might have less than honorable intentions, I declined and said I would see him in the morning. I was a little sharp with him, and after I hung up, I felt bad about it. He was not from the South, and I thought that, like Larry, he might also be feeling out of place. About three minutes later, the phone rang again. It was the same guy, saying that he really did need to talk to me that night and it wouldn't take long. Thinking I might have misjudged him, I relented and told him he could come up.

I should have followed my first instinct, because as soon as he entered my room and closed the door, he removed every stitch of clothing he was wearing. I was embarrassed and frightened. He was hardly the Adonis of show business, and there was an element of icky self-loathing to his exhibitionism. I started edging toward the door. He wondered why I was so shocked. Wasn't I a hippie? Didn't hippies believe in free love? In case this wasn't enough to impress me, he mentioned that he could make things go well for me in the television business. Thinking how little I liked performing on television, I rolled my eyes and told him I was leaving and that he had better be gone when I returned, or I would call hotel security. He said no one would believe me because of the way I looked and dressed (jeans, long, straight hair, and no bra in the panty-girdle, big-hair South).

Then he said that no one on the show would believe me either, so I had better keep my mouth shut, or he would make things very unpleasant for me.

I went out the door and downstairs to sit in the tiny Ramada Inn lobby, where I felt bored, annoyed, and sleepy. After about an hour, I went back, found my room empty, and put the chain on the door. I called Herb and told him what had happened. He was furious at the guy from his office for leaving me alone in Nashville. He decided that it would stir up trouble if we complained about the producer, and I was likely to be dropped from the show. Herb felt the best way to handle it was to act like it didn't happen, and he sent another person to help me for the rest of the time that I had to be there. The next morning at the read-through, the man who had been in my room turned to me and said for everyone to hear, "I left my watch in your room last night. Could you get it for me later?" I don't remember his name, only that he was soon to be married. I felt sorry for his bride-to-be.

The next few years were difficult. I felt I was floundering as a singer and my style hadn't jelled. In 1969 I opened for Jerry Jeff Walker at the Bitter End in Greenwich Village. Jerry Jeff, probably best known for writing the classic "Mr. Bojangles," a song about an old street dancer he'd met in a New Orleans jail, was accompanied by one other guitar player, David Bromberg, a musician of eclectic brilliance and great sensitivity. I continue to revere David as a songwriter, provocative performer, and cherished friend. In those days, I was much taken by his youthful, earnest sincerity. He came to me one night after the show and said I must go with him to the nearby Cafe Au Go-Go to hear his friend Gary White. He said White had written some good songs, and there was one in particular that he felt would be perfect for me. I was prepared to be disappointed. I thought it difficult for someone else to know what I looked for in a song.

At the Cafe Au Go-Go, Gary was playing backup guitar for songwriter Paul Siebel. We saw the last part of his very impressive show made rich with his cowboy falsetto and a song about a poignant, sad girl of a certain reputation named Louise, and then went backstage to meet Gary. He had already packed up his guitar, so he took it back out of its case, sat down, and began to sing a song called "Long Long Time." I told Gary I wanted to record it immediately.

At that time, my producer was Elliot Mazer, who eventually produced albums by Neil Young, and had already recorded with Jerry Jeff Walker, Gordon Lightfoot, Richie Havens, and Ian and Sylvia. He worked closely with a group of studio musicians from Nashville called Area Code 615. Weldon Myrick, the pedal steel player, had an electronic device on his instrument that generated a sound he called the Goodlettsville String Quartet. When combined with Buddy Spicher's violin playing the top note of the chord, it sounded like a gritty orchestra string section. It was an unusual sound for the time, with a touching emotional quality. Norbert Putnam, the bass player, quickly organized the arrangement. I thought the musicians played it beautifully. I never liked my performance on the record. It was recorded at ten in the morning, somewhat early for a singer, and we used the live vocal. I learned to sing it better later. It was a big hit for me in 1970, and it bought me time to learn.

I went back to New York to reconnect with David, Gary, and Jerry Jeff, and find some more songs. I was introduced to Eric Kaz, who taught me a song he wrote with Libby Titus called "Love Has No Pride." We made the rounds of the then current hangouts in Greenwich Village: the Dugout, Nobody's, the Tin

Angel. We saw Paul Siebel perform again at the Cafe Au Go-Go. We took Paul with us and spent the rest of the night at Gary's little apartment in the Village playing music. He taught me how to play the song about the ill-fated Louise: "Well, they all said Louise was not half bad / It was written on the walls and windowpanes."

At dawn, Jerry Jeff and I shared a cab back uptown. Jerry Jeff's face was barely visible in the gray light when he turned to me and said, "I heard these two sisters from Canada sing at the Philadelphia Folk Festival. They wrote a beautiful song you should hear." He bent his head low, closed his eyes, and softly sang for me all he could remember of the song:

> Some say a heart is just like a wheel
> When you bend it
> You can't mend it
> And my love for you is like a sinking ship
> And my heart is on that ship out in mid-ocean

I felt like a bomb had exploded in my head. Even in those few lines I could tell that the song, both plainspoken and delicate, had a highly original approach to describing the deadly peril of romantic love. I begged him to ask them to send me a recording of it. It arrived in my mailbox a few weeks later on a reel-to-reel tape. Titled "Heart Like a Wheel," it was written by Anna McGarrigle, and she sang it with her sister Kate. It rearranged my entire musical landscape.

The McGarrigles defied categorization and were not understood by all. Not exactly pop music composers, they sprang more from the artistic bloodline of American composer John Jacob Niles, and, along with fellow Canadian Leonard Cohen, have made a significant contribution to the world of American art song. They soldiered on amidst a pop music world devoted to exploring the concepts of bigger and louder, tougher and more disaffected, and planted their musical flag in an emotional realm of unabashed sentiment and artless candor. A line from "The Work Song," one of my favorites of their early compositions, says, "Label it garbage, label it art. / You couldn't call it soul, you had to call it heart."

They wrote heart music, indeed.

Onstage, their sibling dynamic made one think of unseparated littermates. In the audience, it felt like we had entered their living room unannounced and discovered them squabbling, working out harmonies, or sweeping up after a boisterous party. They wore odd clothing, even by show business standards. Canadians are quite different from Americans and I have always thought that, where clothing is concerned, they are more invested in quality, while we are more invested in glamour. This can make their tweeds and hand-knitted sweaters (things I adore) seem stodgy.

The two of them onstage pressed whatever musical agenda they pleased and seemed completely unconcerned about the framework of a professional show. They never failed to move people, and profoundly. I remember sitting next to my pal John Rockwell at a club in New York City listening to them sing their devastating song "Talk to Me of Mendocino." I was already blubbering into my root beer float and looked sideways at John. What I saw was a seasoned and highly discriminating music critic from *The New York Times* with two large tears rolling down his face.

Their children continue what they started. The most notable among them are Martha and Rufus Wainwright, two singers who, like their mother, Kate, and their Aunt Anna, never fail to make me cry. When the extended families of McGarrigles and Wainwrights give a concert, which they will do occasionally, it is like being caught in a genetic whirlwind of talent and inspiration.

Kate and Anna opened a door for me, and I scooted through it as fast as I could.

4

California Country Rock

*Playing the Palomino Club in Los
Angeles: Ed Black on guitar, Mickey
McGhee on drums.*

BACK IN LOS ANGELES, I continued to look for musicians who
would be sympathetic to the new songs I was finding. I put together a band with Bernie Leadon and Jeff Hanna, who was on
hiatus from the Nitty Gritty Dirt Band. They called themselves
the Corvettes. We played some shows around the country, but
eventually Jeff went back to the Dirt Band and Bernie joined
the Flying Burrito Brothers. Jeff, one of the friendliest, sweetest
guys in the music business, introduced me to Steve Martin, who
had the same manager as the Dirt Band, Bill McEuen. He was

the brother of the band's dazzling multi-instrumentalist, John McEuen. We all wound up playing various shows together, some at the Troubadour, and some at the Boarding House in San Francisco. When we weren't onstage we would watch Steve perform his brilliant early material: Balloon Animals, The Great Flydini, The Cruel Shoes, Arrow Through the Head. No one had achieved any great success in those days. Steve was just our pal, and we thought he was hilarious.

Bernie and I both lived north of Los Angeles in Topanga Canyon, so I spent a lot of time hanging out with him. I watched him hone his country rock guitar style by going to school on Merle Haggard. Every morning, Bernie would put on a pot of coffee, plug in his red Gibson ES-335 semi-hollow-body guitar, and drop the needle on the latest Haggard record. It was a double album called *Same Train, A Different Time*, and it was a tribute to Jimmie Rodgers. He learned all the guitar parts, and I learned the harmonies sung by Merle's wife, Bonnie Owens. We learned all the other Merle Haggard records too, plus George Jones and Tammy Wynette.

Bernie still played in my band when he had time off from the Burrito Brothers, and one night we performed on a TV show called *Playboy After Dark*. After we finished the show, we went to the Troubadour to see what was going on at the bar. We ran into Bernie's Burrito bandmate Gram Parsons. He said he was going to the Chateau Marmont, a Hollywood hotel where he was in residence, to play some music. He wanted us to come along. We got in Bernie's car, and Gram directed us up a winding road in the Hollywood Hills to a large modern house that was definitely not the Chateau Marmont. When we went inside, we were introduced to Keith Richards. The Rolling Stones were in town putting the finishing touches on *Let It Bleed*, and Keith and Mick Jagger had rented a house for the time they would be working in Los Angeles.

Gram and Keith had struck up a friendship over Keith's interest in learning about country music. We got down to business immediately and sang all the Merle Haggard songs we knew. Gram was singing lead, and Bernie and I added the harmony parts. Keith was playing guitar and soaking up everything Gram had to show him. All good musicians learn from one another this way. After a few hours, Bernie noticed it was two in the morning and said he needed to make the long drive back to Topanga Canyon. I had moved to Hollywood by then, and he said he would drop me off. Gram twisted his choirboy face into a pout and asked if I would stay and go through the George Jones repertoire. Jones's material was based on duets with Tammy Wynette, so we could sing them without Bernie supplying the third part. Gram assured me that he could take me home because my house was close to the Chateau Marmont. I stayed. We went through George Jones, and then Keith played "Wild Horses," a new song that he and Mick had just written.

Gram was salivating over this song and begged Keith to let him record it before the Rolling Stones did. This was a bold request, as writers who record don't usually give up a song before they release it themselves. I was surprised when they allowed him to use it on the next Flying Burrito Brothers record, a year before they would include their own version on the album *Sticky Fingers*. I wanted the song too but knew I wasn't going to have it.

It was about five in the morning, so I asked Gram if he could take me home as promised. He knit up his brow. "You see, dearie," he said (Gram called people dearie, maybe because he was condescending to me, maybe because he grew up in the South, or maybe a little of both), "I only have my motorcycle up here, and I'd have to take you home on it." I blanched. I wasn't about to climb on a motorcycle with Gram in any condition, and his had deteriorated considerably after Bernie left. I hadn't been smoking the joint they were passing back and forth. I had tried marijuana several times, but in the words of my friend and long-time assistant Janet Stark, "When I smoke pot, it makes me want to hide under the bed with a box of graham crackers and *not* share." I didn't have any objections to them smoking but knew it didn't get you as loaded as Gram seemed to be when he came back from one of his little excursions out of the room.

It had been a long night, and at about six, we went into the kitchen to see if we could find something to eat. Gram hoisted himself up on the kitchen counter and began to sing something, except we couldn't make out what it was. He was swaying in a large circle from his perch on the counter, and I was afraid he would fall and hurt himself. He was talking, but we had no idea what he was saying. I had never seen anyone in his condition. Keith and I hauled him off the counter, wrapped his arms around our shoulders, and helped him back to the living room. We lowered him down on one of the sofas, where he passed out, saying something about a blinky. I took it to mean that he was cold and covered him with a blanket.

Keith moved under his own steam to the next horizontal surface and proceeded to dreamland. That left me sitting for the next several hours, still in my itchy television makeup, wishing for my flannel nightgown. There was nothing to do but wait until ten o'clock when Herb's office opened, and I could call and ask someone to come and get me. I never went to another all-night jam session without my own very sober ride home.

In the spring of 1970, I met two people in the Troubadour who would become important to me later. One was David Geffen, the former college roommate of my Hart Street pal, *Beverly Hillbillies* TV writer Ron Pearlman. David introduced himself to me one evening, and I found him to be as Ron had described, with a saucy sense of humor and a restless, penetrating intelligence. He had a cozy manner, a confidential way of conversing, and unrelenting, irresistible charm. He and his former William Morris mailroom coworker Elliot Roberts became Troubadour regulars. Keen observers, they started a management company and assembled an impressive stable of thoroughbreds. It included Laura Nyro; Joni Mitchell; Neil Young; Crosby, Stills, and Nash; and, eventually, Jackson Browne, the Eagles, and John David Souther. David went on to form a hugely successful label called Asylum Records.

The other person was John Boylan. John was introduced to me as the man who had produced the latest single for Rick Nelson, "She Belongs to Me." In addition to being a big seller, the record was tasteful and thoughtfully produced. John had helped put together a band to back Nelson called the Stone Canyon Band. It featured steel guitar legend Buddy Emmons, plus a number of L.A. country rock stalwarts. It sounded like my dream band. I asked him if he would consider putting together a band for me, and he agreed.

John stood with the best of the grownups among the Troubadour regulars. As a young man in his twenties, he had a head of thick, gray hair, and faded blue eyes to confirm his Irish surname. He was smart, well behaved, and well educated, with a degree in theater arts from Bard College. He knew his way around a stage, and he knew his way around the music business. He was a healthy specimen, slender and fit. We called him Fat John. He produced some recordings for me, and we started to build a touring band.

I was living with John David Souther on Camrose Place, which was a little court of bungalows on the hill below the Hollywood Bowl amphitheater. He had the flint-eyed, dusty-wind squint of the Texas Panhandle, where he had been raised. When

I met John David he was playing drums for Bo Diddley, but it was his songwriting that impressed me.

Jackson Browne lived in the bungalow adjacent to us. Jackson was younger than most of us by a couple of years, but he always ran in front of the pack. In the Troubadour community of blistering raw talent, he was a little smarter, a little further evolved in his thinking, a little more refined in his writing practice. He could use his relatively small voice to great advantage. Jackson has a Doppler effect way of starting a musical phrase that seems to be coming from far away at great speed. It builds in intensity till it disappears in the distance, leaving the listener sprawling. He was sixteen when I met him on Hart Street, shortly after I had arrived in Los Angeles, and he had already written "These Days," a beautifully crafted song that stands with his best.

Later, we toured together, often alternating as headliner, depending on who had the bigger regional hit. In our little circle, Jackson was touched earliest by tragedy. His beautiful young wife, Phyllis, who was a troubled girl long before they met, committed suicide, leaving him a small child to raise. Jackson, devastated, did his best to step up to the task. I remember him and his little son running up and down the aisle of our tour bus. Jackson had a beach towel tied around his neck to resemble Superman's cape, trying to make touring life seem like it was something normal—trying to ransom his boy's childhood from the fate he'd been dealt by the death of his mother.

John David Souther and Glenn Frey had been a duo called Longbranch Pennywhistle, and they spent a lot of time with Jackson, swapping ideas and writing songs together. Warren Zevon, with his literate, quirky sensibility, was also included. I never got to know Warren well. I remember him as someone who mostly stayed quiet, his complicated gaze directed at the floor.

He was the only person I ever knew with a subscription to *Jane's Defence Weekly*. There was a lot of competition among those individuals, with no lack of silverback posturing, yet I always had the sense that they admired and respected one another's work, and weren't stingy about giving support and encouragement.

I recently came across an old cassette tape recorded in my living room in Malibu, sometime around 1976, of Jackson teaching me to sing Zevon's "Poor Poor Pitiful Me," plugging a song for his buddy whose writing he so admired. Listening to the tape, I wonder why Jackson didn't record it himself, because he sang it better than I did. Later on in the tape, John David teaches me Roy Orbison's "Blue Bayou," which also made it onto the *Simple Dreams* album. That was a profitable evening.

After time on the road with Herb Cohen as my manager, I was beginning to feel some wear and tear. Herb was known for not pampering his artists. He would tell me in the bluntest terms when he thought I was out of line or getting an exaggerated sense of my own importance. Most artists, and especially girl singers, can wind up living comfortably at the center of their own universe, and I am grateful for the efforts he made to restrain this tendency—even though they weren't always successful. When he would look at me in exasperation and say, "Linda, you're full of shit," he was usually right. Unfortunately, he didn't know much about music, and his keen instincts didn't include an ability to even guess what goes into making it. More troubling to me was the fact that his business practices were somewhat irregular.

One afternoon, John Boylan and I were sitting in Herb's office when a call came through from Capitol Records. We could hear only his side of the conversation, but it was something about me being invited to sing at the 1970 Capitol Records sales convention, along with Glen Campbell, then at his peak of popularity as host of his own weekly musical variety show, and the great jazz saxophonist Cannonball Adderley. The convention would be held in Hawaii, and we would have all our expenses paid first class to Honolulu. I remember Herb telling the fellow from Capitol that it would be easier if they just sent him the money, and he could buy the tickets out of his office, not an unreasonable request.

The night before we left for Hawaii, we had played a concert in San Jose, so the tickets we had from Herb's travel agent were for a flight leaving from San Francisco. We were pretty excited about going to Hawaii, and even more excited about flying first class. As we approached the boarding gate, we noticed a few police officers standing nearby. It turned out that they were interested in talking to us. We were traveling with a fiddle player, Gib Guilbeau, and I played a second fiddle part on some of the songs. We both carried our instruments on the planes so that they wouldn't be smashed by the baggage handlers. I thought the police might have suspected that we were concealing weapons in our violin cases. I opened mine to show that it really did contain a violin, but that was not their concern. Herb's office had given our tickets to John, and when he'd handed them to the person at the boarding gate, they matched the numbers on tickets that had been reported stolen. The police arrested us and took us directly to the San Mateo County Jail. At first it seemed funny to all of us, and as long as I was with the rest of the band, I wasn't too concerned. Of course, as soon as we arrived at the jail, I, being the only female, was taken to a separate facility.

Herb and his wife had left a few days before us and were already enjoying the sun in Honolulu. Also, it was a Sunday, so there wasn't anyone at his office. I called Herb's brother, Martin Cohen, at home and explained what had happened. He was a lawyer who handled all Herb's legal affairs. It took him most of the day to find a bail bondsman to get us out of there. I was freezing to death in the Levi's shorts and sandals I had worn for the beach in Hawaii, and the jail matrons were making fun of my Porky Pig T-shirt. John and the band were in the drunk tank under more crowded and sinister conditions, but at least they were together. After we were bailed out, John took us back to the airport and bought new first-class tickets on his American Express card.

When we finally got to Hawaii, we found out that both the band Santana and singer Eric Burdon had been arrested at other airports on the same day for the same reason, and they were using the same travel agency. Herb said he used that agency because it gave him huge discounts on tickets. He insisted that he hadn't known they were stolen. I wondered what he had meant to do with the difference between the money he had received from Capitol and what he paid for the hot tickets, but I didn't ask him. It was not different from the way many people operated in the music business. But I knew my father would not do business in this way. It bothered me.

In Hawaii, we were introduced to Cannonball Adderley and his brother, Nat, the jazz trumpeter and cornet player. They were very sympathetic to our tales of false accusation and incarceration. We spent some time listening to them play in the hotel room, and then, in the evening, Nat and I went walking by a lagoon and talked for a long time about music. It was the opposite of being in jail. I loved a Frank Loesser song his brother had recorded in 1961 with singer Nancy Wilson, called "Never Will I Marry." She was barely out of her teens when she recorded it, and it was a stunning performance. I admired it for years and finally sang the song on *Hummin' to Myself*, an album I recorded in 2004.

I confided in John that I was not happy with Herb's wrecking-ball management style, and he urged me to see what other management situation I could find.

I had recently met Peter Asher in New York when he and his wife, Betsy, had come to see me at the Bitter End. Peter's experience in the business was deep and varied, and he was one of the rare individuals who understood the music as well as the business. Born in London, Peter had begun his long career as a child actor in the British theater, and had worked regularly both onstage and in film and television. After his preadolescent stint singing in a boys' choir, he became enormously successful as one half of the duo Peter and Gordon, which he had formed with his school chum Gordon Waller. His sister, Jane Asher, herself a highly regarded stage and film actress, became sweethearts with Paul McCartney during the days of the Beatles' early success, and Paul wrote four of Peter and Gordon's biggest hits, including "Woman" and "A World Without Love." A few years later, when the Beatles decided to form their own recording label, Apple Records, they enlisted Peter to head their A&R (Artists and Repertoire) department. He signed James Taylor to the label, then later left Apple and moved to the United States, where he became James's manager and producer.

Betsy was a good cook and a sympathetic listener. She and Peter gave lovely dinner parties. Jackson Browne, John Boylan, Carole King, James Taylor, Joni Mitchell, Don Henley, John David, and I were among the regulars at Peter and Betsy's cozy dinners. Boylan suggested that I ask Peter to manage me, and I told Herb I was going to end our professional relationship. This was not so easy, as I had just signed a five-year contract with him.

We hired lawyers and went to an endless, boring deposition. Herb and I rolled our eyes and giggled with each other even though we were supposed to be on opposite sides. During our lunch break, we went to eat together, and he suggested to me that the lawsuit would drag on forever and be weighted in his favor because his brother was his lawyer and his legal bills would be far less costly than mine. "Linda," he said insistently, "if we could agree on a figure, it would save us from having to sit in boring depositions, and the money you'll end up paying to a lawyer could just go straight to me." We agreed on an amount and shook hands. It took me a couple of years to pay him off, but we parted on good terms. I was sad because I was genuinely fond of Herb and still consider him one of the more interesting characters I met in the music business, but I needed someone who understood music and took a more gentlemanly approach in his business dealings. Peter Asher was a gentleman to his core.

John made an appointment with Peter and went with me to ask him to manage me. Peter agreed to do so. But a few weeks later, he called me over to his house to tell me that because he had already agreed to manage James's sister, singer Kate Taylor, also managing me could create a conflict of interest that might be unfair to both of us—and so he would have to decline. I was disappointed, and John, who was a record producer and not a manager, agreed to fill in until I could make other arrangements.

The Eagles founding members: (left to right) Bernie Leadon, Randy Meisner, Don Henley, Glenn Frey.

5

The Eagles

JOHN BOYLAN AND I were at a Troubadour Hoot Night one evening, scouting musicians to back me up, when a Texas band called Shiloh began to play and stopped us in our tracks. They were playing my arrangement of "Silver Threads and Golden Needles," and they were playing it really well. I was impressed by the drummer, who was a strong player with a lean, unfussy style. Better still, he seemed to have an awareness of the rhythm traditions of country music, which included the subtler, unamplified styles of bluegrass and old-time string band music. This was rare for rock drummers, who often hammered over the delicate nuances of traditional songs and rhythms, draining them of their charm. This made him ideal for playing with a singer.

John introduced himself and asked him if he would like to play some shows we had coming up at the Cellar Door, a club in the Georgetown section of Washington, D.C. The drummer's name was Don Henley. Bernie Leadon was busy with the Burrito Brothers, so I asked John David's Longbranch Pennywhistle partner Glenn Frey if he would come along and play guitar. We added a bass player and a lead guitarist, and Boylan played keyboards.

In those days, we couldn't afford to get single rooms for everyone, so the guys had to double up. Glenn wound up rooming with Don and discovered why Don played so well for singers. It turned out that Don was a singer himself, and a good one. Like

Glenn, he was also an accomplished songwriter, and the two began playing music all night and ignited a musical friendship. Glenn referred to Don as the "secret weapon" and said that they had decided to form a band together.

John offered to help them and suggested that they continue to tour with me while they were waiting to get a record deal and gigs of their own. That way they would have an income, and I would have a solid band for several months. John suggested they get Randy Meisner to play bass. Randy had just recently left Rick Nelson's Stone Canyon Band and John thought he was a strong bass player and a great high-harmony singer. I suggested Bernie Leadon, also a strong singer, to play guitar. They liked one another and started to work together right away.

One day they needed a place to rehearse their vocal parts. John David offered the living room of our little house on Camrose Place. The room wasn't very big, so we went out to the movies to give them some space. When we walked in a few hours later, they sounded fantastic. They had worked out a four-part-harmony arrangement of a song that Bernie and Don wrote and had spent some time getting their vocal blend just right. In that small room, with only acoustic guitars and four really powerful voices, the sound was huge and rich. They called the new song "Witchy Woman." I was sure it was going to be a hit.

6

Beachwood Drive

Photo by Henry Diltz.

JOHN DAVID AND I moved into an apartment on North Beachwood Drive, under the Hollywood sign. We took it over from Warren Zevon and his girlfriend, Tule, who needed space for their small child. It was in a charming Mediterranean building, constructed in the 1920s, with large Palladian windows that bathed our living room in California sunshine. The apartment had battered hardwood floors, a wood-burning fireplace, and enough room for John David's baby grand piano. MGM Studios had a sale, and I bought some old lace curtains that had been used on one of its movie sets and hung them on the windows.

There were four units in the apartment complex. Harry Dean Stanton, the actor, lived in the back over the garage. He and I struck up a friendship right away because he loved the Mexican huapangos that I knew, and he had learned to sing and play them on his guitar. Sometimes we would go watch him perform them at McCabe's, the performing space managed by my old Stone Poneys' bandmate, Bob Kimmel.

Lawrence "Stash" Wagner, guitarist for the group Fraternity of Man, lived with his wife and child in the tiny ground floor unit. He had cowritten that immortal song with Elliot Ingber, featured in the Dennis Hopper film *Easy Rider*, "Don't Bogart That Joint."

John David and I lived on the top floor, and comedy writer Bill Martin, who later went on to a long career as a TV writer and producer, lived directly below us. Bill coined a phrase when he wrote a deeply philosophical song called "The Whole Enchilada Marches On." He was a funny guy who hid an alert intelligence behind a half-lidded, slow-moving exterior. His apartment was fitted out with the latest hippie essentials. He had a great stereo system with big speakers, a beanbag chair, and a water pipe. He and his wife had a knack for horticulture and grew their own incredibly strong marijuana in terra-cotta pots.

They took pride in their hospitality. This consisted of settling a guest comfortably in the beanbag chair, playing Otis Redding loud enough to induce hemorrhage, and pounding paralyzing doses of marijuana in a water pipe. With the guests immobilized by cannabis, Bill would tell a story of the grisly murder that had apparently been committed in their apartment before they occupied it. At the story's climax, he would flip back the rug to show a large bloodstain that had never come out of the floor.

John David and I, both avid readers, were happy to have the quietest space in our little complex, where we could hole up with our books and our music. He wrote a lot of good songs in that apartment, including "Faithless Love," "Prisoner in Disguise," and "Simple Man, Simple Dream," all of which I would later record.

I played the Dutch housewife, scrubbing and applying layers of wax to the floors, trying to coax a shine out of the old floorboards that had seen too many generations of indifferent housekeeping. While waiting for the wax to harden, I worked out my guitar parts to new songs I liked. By the time the floor was gleaming, I had the song learned.

Sometimes the doubts and fears that were generated by trying to create something of our own would circle us in a menacing way, and we would seek safety in the recordings of some of our most revered music masters. It was a great pleasure to float around in these little pools of perfection, happy to be relieved of the intimidating task of trying to invent them ourselves. Some of the standout recorded performances I remember listening to with him were "Drown in My Own Tears" on the *Ray Charles in Person* album, Brahms's Trio in B Major played by cellist Pablo Casals, and Donny Hathaway's masterful rendition of the John Lennon classic "Jealous Guy." These were bricks that we tried to cement into our musical basements.

One album always seemed to finish up the evening, and we would play the whole thing straight through. It set a devastating mood and required strict concentration from start to finish. This was *Frank Sinatra Sings for Only the Lonely,* the record I had first heard at Alan Fudge's house in Tucson. I learned some beautiful songs from that recording, including "What's New," the title song from the first collection of American standard songs that I eventually recorded with Sinatra's arranger, Nelson Riddle.

John David was a great listening partner. The pleasure and learning experience of hearing music increases exponentially when done with someone of a deeply shared sensibility. Years later, the head of my record label thought that I was throwing away my career by wanting to record "What's New," with a full orchestra and a jazz band. John David understood what I was chasing, and he encouraged me.

After about a year and a half, John David moved to a house a few blocks away. We remained friends but had drifted into different webs of our own needs and interests. He was writing a lot, and I was traveling nonstop. We've always had feelings of affection and sympathy for each other. I still want to know about the songs he's just written.

The last shows I played with the Eagles as my official backup band were at Disneyland in 1971 for a week of end-of-school-year festivities called Grad Night. We were on a bill with Smokey Robinson and the Miracles, plus the Staple Singers. The Disney Company paid well but had many particular requirements of the talent it booked in the park. We played several shows a night, finished up around three in the morning, and weren't allowed to wander through the park in between shows. Also, our contract stipulated that I was required to wear a bra, and my skirt had to be a certain number of inches from the ground while I was kneeling.

When no one was onstage performing, the Eagles played poker with Smokey and the Miracles in the backstage artists' lounge. I prissed around the room hoping to get Smokey to notice me. He didn't. It would be hard to overstate the impact of Smokey Robinson's magnetism. First of all, there are his beautiful gray-green eyes. After that is his cool flame of devastating charm that makes women sigh and men admire. Failing to impress him in any way, I went home and started learning his songs. A few years later, I had big hits with two songs that he wrote, "The Tracks of My Tears" and "Ooh Baby Baby." He invited me to sing them with him on the Motown twenty-fifth anniversary television special in 1983, which also featured Michael Jackson singing "Billie Jean" and performing the moonwalk for the first time in front of a national audience. Smokey was unfailingly supportive and gracious, but my knees were knocking together. Singing "Ooh Baby Baby" while staring into Smokey's eyes was both intimidating and exhilarating, and remains one of the highest peaks of my career. In 2009 I listened to Smokey speaking as one musician to another in a most encouraging, inclusive, and generous way as he gave the commencement address to the graduating class of the Berklee College of Music. We were both awarded honorary doctorates.

By late 1972, John Boylan had helped me to build a solid following performing at colleges, but my records seemed to have hit a discouraging plateau, both artistically and commercially. I was running in one direction trying to please the record company, and in another one trying to please myself. I had been trying to interest the people at Capitol in letting me record "Heart Like a Wheel," but they saw no commercial potential for it. They wanted me to work with a Bakersfield-style country producer. I thought some good records had come out of Bakersfield, particularly Merle Haggard's, but I didn't feel that the style had anything to do with my more eclectic aspirations.

I owed Capitol only one more record. Offers were already coming in from heads of other labels, including Clive Davis at Columbia, Mo Ostin at Warner Bros., and Albert Grossman at his new label, Bearsville. Grossman was Bob Dylan's manager and he also handled the careers of Peter, Paul and Mary, the Band, and Janis Joplin. The best offer was from David Geffen at his new company, Asylum Records. It was a small label, and its few artists would get a lot of personalized attention. John had spearheaded a successful attempt to get the Eagles signed to Asylum, and it was rapidly becoming a home to singer-songwriters and the L.A. country rock sound, including Jackson Browne, Joni Mitchell, J. D. Souther, and Judee Sill. I knew I would be in the company of other like-minded artists.

Geffen felt that I could lose the momentum I'd gained if I put out another record that wasn't promoted properly by a team that understood the direction I was trying to take with my music. He said he thought I should ask Capitol to let him have the next record, and it could have the one after that.

John arranged a meeting with Bhaskar Menon, who was then president of Capitol. I felt a little embarrassed meeting Menon. Herb Cohen had tried unsuccessfully to get me released from Capitol earlier. He had threatened Menon with bad public behavior on my part that could put Capitol in a bad light. It was a bluff, because I hadn't agreed to any such thing, and it was precisely that kind of artist-as-battering-ram management style that had made me leave Herb. He also encouraged me to think of Menon as the enemy. I had never met him before and was surprised to find a charming, refined, and intelligent gentleman from India with beautiful manners. His sensitive, kindly demeanor was quite a change from the cigar-chomping, hookers-and-cocaine American record industry men I had come to see as a defining stereotype. I listened quietly while my attorney, Lee Phillips, spoke for me. Menon replied that they would like to keep me on the label, suggesting that I needed to choose whether to sing rock or country. I didn't want to choose. And I wanted to sing "Heart Like a Wheel."

Menon seemed unpersuaded by Lee Phillips's skillful presentation, so I decided to speak up for myself. I said, "Please, Mr. Menon, let me go. I don't want to be here, I don't fit here, and, besides, you don't need me. You have two other female singers, Helen Reddy and Anne Murray, selling lots of records for you. Let me go!" To our collective surprise, he relented. I was free to sign with Geffen.

7

Neil Young Tour

Photo by Henry Diltz.

IN JANUARY 1973 DAVID Geffen called John Boylan and said that
he wanted me to join the upcoming Neil Young tour as the opening act. I was reluctant, to say the least, because my show and
my band were set up to play small clubs, and our first concert
with Neil was going to be at Madison Square Garden. David and
John knew what a boost the huge exposure to audiences across
the country would give my record sales, and they talked me into it.
With just a few days' notice, we were off to New York City.

That night, a few songs into Neil's set, someone handed him a
note saying that National Security Adviser Henry Kissinger had
reached an agreement in Paris ending the United States's involve-
ment in Vietnam. Neil announced simply, "The war is over." The
audience of eighteen thousand exploded, cheering, crying, and

screaming for the next ten minutes. In the middle of all the pande-monium, I was huddled in a corner wrestling with the fact that I was still a club act with a not very loud kind of folky band, no dis-cernible stage patter, and no clue how to reach a crowd like that.

I changed backup singers, stage clothes, and attitudes for three months (seventy-eight shows), as we worked our way back west across the country. I was encouraged nightly by the side stage presence of Neil's piano player, Jack Nitzsche, who, in addition to being a really good piano player, was a really mean drunk. He told me with metronomic regularity that as a singer and performer, I was not up to the task of opening for Neil, and that he was going to talk Neil into hiring soul singer Claudia Lennear or singer-songwriter Jackie DeShannon to replace me. Even though I basically shared his opinion, I wasn't going to let a mean drunk shove me off the stage, and I continued to see what I could do to improve. I also watched Neil, who was nothing but nice to me, play his show every single night, and I continue to find him one of the purest singers and most uniquely gifted songwriters in contemporary music. Hearing his eerie, prairie-wind howl of a voice—a boy soprano fuel-injected with testosterone—in such regular and concentrated doses was a huge part of my musical education and an enduring pleasure.

The tour was traveling in a chartered Lockheed Electra tur-boprop airliner. On board were assorted managers, Neil's band, my band, and a few members of the sound crew. The stewardess was Linda Keith, who was married to Neil's pedal steel player, Ben Keith. She did her job with friendly efficiency and appeared cheerfully unaware of the substances that were being ignited or hoovered by some of the passengers during the flights. I was happy that she also kept us supplied with fresh fruit. She prob-ably saved us from scurvy.

In late February, we landed at Houston Intercontinental

Airport. We were booked for a concert at the Sam Houston Coliseum, a ten-thousand-seat hockey arena, with the following night off in Houston before we pushed on to Kansas City, Missouri. When we got to the hotel, we ran into Eddie Tickner, who was Gram Parsons's manager. He told us that Gram and Emmylou Harris, the new girl he was singing with, were playing at a well-known Houston honky-tonk called Liberty Hall.

Chris Hillman of the Byrds, and later Gram's bandmate in the Flying Burrito Brothers, had told me one night that he and Gram had met Emmylou in Washington, D.C., and loved her singing. He said he felt we really needed to meet each other—that we were pursuing similar ideas in our music—and he was certain we would like each other. I was excited to get the chance to experience for myself what Chris had been talking about and asked John Boylan if he would make arrangements for the two of us to see their show after we finished playing ours that night.

We arrived at Liberty Hall to find it filled with members of a club called the Sin City Boys. They were plenty rowdy, but when Gram and Emmylou started to sing, it got very quiet. Clearly, something unusual was taking place up on that stage, and we in the audience were mesmerized. Emmy has the ability to make each phrase of a song sound like a last desperate plea for her life, or at least her sanity. No melodrama; just the plain truth of raw emotion. The sacred begging the profane.

My reaction to it was slightly conflicted. First, I loved her singing wildly. Second, in my opinion, she was doing what I was trying to do, only a whole lot better. Then came a split-second decision I made that affected the way I listened to and enjoyed music for the rest of my life. I thought that if I allowed myself to become envious of Emmy, it would be painful to listen to her, and I would deny myself the pleasure of it. If I simply surrendered to loving what she did, I could take my rightful place among the other drooling Emmylou fans, and then maybe, just maybe, I might be able to sing with her.

I surrendered.

Back at the hotel, we told Neil about what a great show it had been. He and his band, the Stray Gators, plus members of my band, went with us the following night. Gram and Emmy did another great show, and Neil and I sat in at the end. Someone had given Gram and Emmy jackets with the words *Sin City* stitched on the back. One of the Sin City Boys came up to the stage and presented one to me. I wore it for years. After the show, the owner of Liberty Hall hosted a party in the big dressing room upstairs.

That's when the trouble started. Jack Nitzsche came over, put his arm around me, and began to speak in a very complimentary way. Then gradually what he said became abusive. I was used to the nightly routine of cutting remarks and tried to move away. Because he was a keyboard player, he had powerful arms and had me locked in a tight grip. He continued to slur the cruelest and most insulting things he could muster in his inebriated state. I asked him to let me go. He said that he was going to make me fight my way out. It became obvious to me that he wanted to make an ugly scene, and I didn't want a big fight with Jack to spoil the wonderful evening we had just had with Gram and Emmy. Still, his mean-spirited bullying had frightened me, and, though I tried hard not to, I began to cry. John Boylan, my drummer, Mickey McGee, and my pedal steel player, Ed Black, noticed from across the room that I was upset, and moved in to help me. With three husky men in my corner, Nitzsche backed off.

We decided to go back to the hotel. Downstairs, there were two or three waiting limos. We climbed into the first one in line and found Gram and his wife, Gretchen, already waiting inside. Just as we began to pull away from the curb, there was a knock on the window, and Jack stumbled into the front seat. He turned around and began talking through the partition. "You're a mess, Gram," he said. "You're fucked up." Gram's reaction was to wonder out loud why the kettle was calling the pot such a deep shade of black. Jack kept at him. "You're a junkie, Gram. You're going to die. Danny Whitten's dead, and you're next," he said, referring to the Crazy Horse guitarist who had died of an overdose just three months before. Gretchen started to cry. Boylan reached forward and closed the partition to shut Jack up.

Gram and Neil wanted to play music some more, so we went to Neil's suite and began to play all the country songs we knew. Emmy wasn't there. We were going through the familiar George Jones, Hank Williams, and Merle Haggard repertoire. Gram and Neil were showing some of their new songs. We were having fun for a while, but Jack went over to the electric keyboard in Neil's room and began pounding nonsense chords. Then he stood up and said, "Your music sucks! I'm going to show you what I think of your music!" He walked over to the middle of the room, unzipped his pants, and began to pee on the floor. Gram threw Jack's hat under the stream, and he wound up peeing in his own hat.

I was out the door. John took me back to my room. I was exhausted and in floods of tears. There was a knock at the door. It was Emmy. She had heard about what had happened with Jack and had come over to try to make me feel better. She brought me a yellow rose. I pressed the rose, and I still have it in a box somewhere. I still have Emmy too.

Years later, after Jack had experienced a period of sobriety, he apologized to me. Looking back, I imagine he genuinely didn't care for my singing, and he was entitled to that. He'd have found me somewhat in agreement, as I was still learning and, in the beginning, way over my head while struggling to perform in those huge arenas. It turned out that I was plenty tough enough to survive the nightly onslaught of his drunken insults. Jack was a stellar musician and arranger, with impressively written arrangements for Phil Spector ("River Deep, Mountain High" by Tina Turner) and the Rolling Stones ("You Can't Always Get What You Want") already to his credit. What I thought was tragic, seeing him act that way, was that he deprived himself of the opportunity to operate in the world with the grace and dignity of which he was fully capable.

The morning after the unfortunate incident in Neil's hotel room, everyone climbed on board the plane and acted like nothing had happened. Someone from Neil's organization must have leaned on Jack and told him to get off my case, because after that, he left me alone. The tour lasted five more weeks. I had a great time.

Six months later, Gram was dead of a drug overdose.

8

Emmylou

Photo by Henry Diltz.

Performing at the
Universal Amphitheater.

I HEARD ABOUT GRAM'S death somewhere on the road, and my immediate concern was for Emmy. I didn't know exactly what the bond between her and Gram consisted of, but I knew it was deep. No one who had seen them sing together would have doubted it.

I called her and could hear in her voice that she was grieving hard. I asked her if she would like to fly out to Los Angeles and spend a little time with me. I had a booking for a week at the Roxy, which was the newest hip Hollywood performing space and bar, founded by Lou Adler and Elmer Valentine, and co-owned by David Geffen, Peter Asher, and Elliot Roberts. I asked her to sit in with my show, thinking it might stir some interest in Emmy as a solo act without Gram.

The first thing she did after she arrived at my apartment was to take out her guitar and play a song she had just written called "Boulder to Birmingham." It brought me to tears and established Emmy as a songwriter to be taken seriously. I was delighted to see she had written such an impressive song, and heartbroken for her about what had inspired it.

We spent a couple of days going through songs that we could harmonize on for the Roxy shows. We worked up a few Hank Williams songs: "I Can't Help It (If I'm Still In Love With You)," and "Honky Tonkin'." Emmy taught me an old song she knew called "The Sweetest Gift (A Mother's Smile)," and we made it into a duet.

When she opened her suitcase, she showed me some clothes she had been given by Nudie, the haute couture fashion designer to all the biggest country-and-western music stars. Nudie and his son-in-law Manuel Cuevas, the brilliant designer from Mexico, had created the suits that Gram and the Flying Burrito Brothers had worn on the cover of their debut album, *The Gilded Palace of Sin*. These clothes were treasures and far too expensive for us to buy. There was a pink Sweetheart of the Rodeo–style jacket that Emmy wore, and a red sparkly vest with white horseshoes on the front that Emmy brought for me to wear. Originally made for country singer Gail Davies, the sparkly vest had short sparkly cuffs to match. I wore them with the Levi's shorts that I had worn to the San Mateo County Jail.

I don't remember much about the shows that we played at the Roxy, only that, in Hollywood, word traveled lightning quick about the beautiful brown-eyed girl with the blazing talent who had been left by Gram Parsons's death to wonder what in the world to do with her musical self. Not too long after that, Emmy signed a recording contract with Warner Bros. Records. The label paired her with Canadian producer Brian Ahern, who assembled the Hot Band to play behind her. It featured some of the finest musicians in Nashville, including Glen D. Hardin from Elvis Presley's band, early rock-and-roll guitar hero James

Burton, and up-and-coming songwriter Rodney Crowell. They made a string of great records together, records that further helped to define country rock as a serious musical discipline.

Back out on the road, we were playing a show in Atlanta, and my band got word that a favorite band of theirs, Little Feat, was playing in a club nearby. I dimly remembered having once met Lowell George, their lead singer and principal songwriter, at my house in Topanga Canyon. I hadn't heard the band. We went to see them after our show, and when we walked in, they were standing on the stage playing "Dixie Chicken." Their Atlanta audience was in a frenzy. Little Feat, to this day my favorite rock-and-roll band, sounded like no other. It had layers of oddly syncopated New Orleans parade beats, with Bill Payne pounding out a keyboard part that conjured the spirits of Professor Longhair, Louis Gottschalk, and Claude Debussy. Sailing over the top of this was Lowell, playing slide guitar with an 11/16 socket wrench from Sears, Roebuck and Co. on his little finger. The socket wrench, heavier than the usual glass bottle top or lipstick tube preferred by blues musicians, gave him a languorous, creamy sound that was completely his own. Lowell had a rich, amber-toned voice that he could whip into and out of falsetto. His blues-saturated vocal embellishments had glimmers of classical Indian singing, and he had unerring pitch and rhythmic savvy. His songwriting style was unrestricted by conventional pop music forms, with quirky lyrics that suggested a prodigious intellect.

Backstage, Lowell walked up to me, opened his fist to reveal a large pill, blinked at me several times, and said, "Hi, want a Quaalude?" No, I didn't want a Quaalude. I wanted to know the open tuning to a song of his, about a truck driver, that he had

sung in the show. He called it "Willin'." We all went to someone's house for a long jam session where Lowell played the song
for me in open G tuning. We soon discovered that for my voice,
it sounded better in the key of E. We agreed to meet when we
were both back home in L.A., and he would show me how to
play it in the new key.

True to his word, Lowell showed up at my apartment with
his big blond Guild acoustic guitar and taught me the song. One
of the problems with changing a song from its original key is that
it can lose the charm of the way the chords are voiced. Also, the
G tuning gains some resonance from having the strings loosened,
or slacked, to make the G chord. Open E tuning is not a slack
key. The relevant strings have to be tuned higher to form the
chord, so it is not as big a sound. Still, the E tuning came roar-
ing out of that big Guild, which he left with me for a few weeks
so that I wouldn't have to retune my own guitar every time I
wanted to play the song. I played it till my fingers blistered.

A few nights before I met Lowell, I was in my room at the
now infamous Watergate Hotel in Washington, D.C., with a
night off and nothing to do. The phone rang. It was Emmy, saying that she was spending the evening with a group of musicians
she felt I just had to get to know, and would I meet her at one
of their houses. She gave me the address and directions to a
place in the suburbs in Bethesda, Maryland. It was the home of
an ear, nose, and throat specialist named John Starling and his
wife, Fayssoux. When John wasn't taking out people's tonsils
in the OR, he played guitar and sang baritone in a bluegrass
band called Seldom Scene. Fayssoux, a speech pathologist, was
a beauty with a cameo profile and shimmering coppery hair to
her waist. She spoke in the refined tones of southern aristocracy,
kept an immaculate home, and was an even more immaculate
harmony singer. She, Emmy, and John had spent countless eve-

nings working up three-part arrangements to traditional songs and country music classics and blended like family when they sang together. There were two other Seldom Scene members: Ben Eldridge, a mathematician, was the banjo player. Mike Auldridge, a graphic artist, played dobro.

Most dobro players have a lot of swagger and growl in their sound, but Mike was an original. Quiet and shy, he approached the music with a kind of hushed reverence that gave his playing an unusual lyrical quality. His was a seminal style that has influenced many younger players, including current dobro virtuoso Jerry Douglas.

We played and sang long into the night, and the next evening I went back and we did it all again. Emmy, who has an infallible ear for a song with integrity, was beginning to explore material for her major label debut record, *Pieces of the Sky*. She played us Billy Sherrill's "Too Far Gone," Felice and Boudleaux Bryant's "Sleepless Nights," and the Stanley Brothers' "Angel Band," John and Fayssoux harmonizing flawlessly. I couldn't wait to get another night off in D.C. so I could sing with them again.

9

Peter Asher

KATE TAYLOR TURNED UP backstage at a show I played with the Eagles at the Capitol Theatre in Passaic, New Jersey. We talked about knitting for a while. She had taught me how to knit woolen socks on five needles, and I told her about the pattern of hearts I had plotted on graph paper and how cool it was to watch the socks take shape. After a while, she changed the subject and told me she no longer wanted a singing career that involved constant touring; she preferred to play music at home and not perform very much. She urged me to ask Peter Asher to manage me again and said she thought he would agree.

We were walking toward a staircase that would take us from the dressing rooms to the stage on the floor below, where the Eagles were beginning their show. I was studying her face closely, to make sure she was comfortable about what she had told me, and I wasn't watching where I was going. I caught my heel on the edge of the top step and tobogganed all the way to the bottom. I had the wind completely knocked out of me, and as I lay in a heap struggling to catch my breath, I made a decision to speak to Peter as soon as I returned to L.A.

Back home in California, I phoned Peter's wife and told her what Kate had said to me. I asked if she thought Peter would still be interested in working with me, and she said she thought it was possible. Why didn't I come for dinner, and we would all discuss it? Betsy made us a casserole out of pork medallions, onions, and potatoes, and we ate it in front of the fire in the dining room of their charming house in Beverly Hills. By the time we got to dessert, we had an agreement. Neither of us wanted a written contract. We sealed the deal with a handshake and a hug.

Having Peter on board meant that John Boylan could go back to doing what he loved most, which was full-time record production. He became a vice president of A&R for Epic Records and produced a series of hits for numerous artists.

By the time Peter and I were able to record together, I had already made *Don't Cry Now* for Asylum and was getting ready to make the album I still owed Capitol. I hadn't played "Heart Like a Wheel" for him because I couldn't bear to see the song rejected again.

One night, I was rehearsing with Andrew Gold, the piano player and guitarist in my band. During a break, he began to play the introduction to "Heart Like a Wheel," and I started to sing it with him. Peter thought it was a beautiful song. The following night, Jackson Browne and I were co-billed to play Carnegie Hall in New York City, so I added it to the show. It got a great response.

My financial ambition for the next tour, slated to begin in January 1974, was simple: I wanted to make enough money to buy a washing machine. Lugging heavy bags full of dirty clothes to the Fluff 'n Fold on the two days I had off before starting another tour was a drag, and I wanted a washing machine almost as much as I had wanted a pony.

The tour was with Jackson Browne, and it was a long one: three months. We had our own bus but could not afford a customized one with sleeping bunks and kitchens. Ours had hard bench seats turned around to face each other. That way we could play endless poker games and music together. We had a lot of overnight trips, so we went to a hardware store and bought pieces of plywood that we used to bridge the seats. We put air mattresses over the plywood and made beds that, in terms of comfort, were only slightly less miserable than sitting up all night. It was two to a bunk, and we climbed in wherever there was a space. The air mattresses all leaked, so in the middle of the night, one of the pair had to blow it back up.

David Lindley was traveling with us, playing with Jackson. David is a multi-instrumentalist who collects and plays a variety of instruments that I can't even pronounce, let alone spell. Still a young man, he had vigorously explored a number of disparate music styles, including Middle Eastern and Central European. David has an elastic face that settles into a puckish expression during the rare times that it is at rest. He is one of the great characters of the music world, with an ability to change accents and personas as readily as he can change instruments and music styles. During one of our conversations, with David Rolodexing through voices and personalities, we discovered that our families are related through my grandmother's grandfather, making him my cousin. I didn't know whether to be delighted or dismayed.

Lacking patience for the two-to-a-berth, leaking-air-mattress arrangement, David had figured out how to sleep in the bus's overhead luggage rack. This space was so tight that it would make a bunk on a submarine seem deluxe. He would emerge from his beauty sleep at odd hours and blast the zydeco music of Louisiana accordionist Clifton Chenier at thundering volume all the way to the back of the bus. No one seemed to mind. David was cherished like a beloved uncle in the late stages of dementia.

Lowell George had a falling out with his bandmates and joined up with us somewhere. He and Jackson sat in the front of the bus night after night while Jackson was writing "Your Bright Baby Blues." Lowell accompanied him on electric slide guitar, which he plugged into a tiny battery-driven Pignose amplifier. Lowell also was writing good songs on that trip. I remember watching him write in a blank book with a Rapidograph pen, carefully printing, in block letters, the lyrics to "Long Distance Love" and "Roll On Through the Night."

We worked our way east to New York City and then turned back south. Meanwhile, the flu epidemic of 1974 was working its way through the passengers on our tour bus. It was a particularly savage virus that year. Some of our band members had been so sick that they had to be left behind, much too weak to travel. By the time we arrived in Washington, D.C., I was coughing, feverish, and could hardly walk. We had a show that night at Georgetown University. Emmy and John Starling came to the show. John took my temperature. It was 103 degrees. I sang anyway but sounded just awful and felt sorry for the audience having to listen to it. John had recently nursed his wife through the same flu. Being a doctor, he knew how dangerous the virus could be and warned me that it could turn into pneumonia. Lowell and I went to stay with John and Fayssoux, and the tour went on without me. I missed the last two shows. That meant no washing machine.

I went to bed and didn't get up for four or five days. When I finally got up, I had only enough strength to go downstairs and lie in the big orange leather beanbag chair in their living room.

In the morning, John put on his white coat and left to see patients and perform surgeries. In the evening, he took off the coat, strapped on his guitar, and played music with Emmylou and members of the Seldom Scene. The first week, I could only lie in the beanbag chair and listen, still too sick to sing. The second week, I began to join in.

Paul Craft, a songwriter friend of John's, came up from Nashville, slept in the Starlings' basement, and taught me to sing his newly written "Keep Me from Blowing Away." I decided to record it there in Maryland and have Paul and John play on it.

John told me about a good sound engineer who had built a great recording studio in nearby Silver Spring. John brought him over to meet me. His name was George Massenburg, and he would eventually become my most important musical partner, working together on at least sixteen albums.

Emmy turned up with her young friend Ricky Skaggs. He was just beginning to develop a name for himself as a formidable bluegrass tenor and superb harmony singer. John Starling had introduced him to Emmy, recommending him for her backup band. I couldn't believe my ears when I heard how well he sang. I sat down with him and started to learn. Over the next ten days, he taught me everything I know about bluegrass harmonies.

Emmy brought a second friend to stay in the Starlings' basement. Jet Thomas had been the dean of freshmen at Harvard, and also a proctor in Gram Parsons's dormitory when Gram studied there in the mid-1960s. Modest and quiet, Jet had piercing blue eyes and a brilliant mind. He and Gram had continued a friendship beyond Harvard, and Jet would appear occasionally at recording sessions and concerts to boost Gram's morale. Emmylou and Jet forged a deep bond of friendship after Gram's death. Jet listened more than he talked, but when he talked, he had a great ability to clarify thinking and change attitudes for the better. In the gravity-defying M. C. Escher landscape of the music business, he was a good man to have around.

With such a great bunch of musicians assembled under one roof, we played all the good songs we knew, and we played all night. Outside it was snowing hard. By midnight, the snow was so deep that no one could leave. Great! We carried on for several more days. Emmy and I have often remarked that we have been recording the songs from our snow marathon for thirty years and counting. They have turned up on my records, Emmy's records, and the Trio records that Emmy and I made with Dolly Parton—usually with George Massenburg presiding in the studio control room.

When the snow was cleared away, we drove to Silver Spring and recorded "Keep Me from Blowing Away." Lowell went along to help and was so impressed with George Massenburg that he patched up his quarrel with Little Feat and talked them into coming to Maryland, where they recorded *Feats Don't Fail Me Now*. Lowell also produced a beautiful album, *Long Time Gone*, for John Starling, with Massenburg engineering on several cuts.

Lowell convinced Massenburg to move to Los Angeles, where he continued to record Little Feat, plus a series of successful albums with Earth, Wind & Fire. He built another studio, the Complex, in West Los Angeles, where Peter Asher and I recorded with him for years.

10
Heart Like a Wheel

PETER AND I BEGAN work on the record I owed Capitol at the Sound Factory in Hollywood in the spring of 1974. The fact that Capitol got to claim that record turned out to be one of the luckiest breaks of my career. Al Coury, one of the best promotion men in the business, was head of A&R and promotion for Capitol. He wanted to show off to upstart David Geffen that he could run a superior sales campaign. It was also in Geffen's interest to have the record sell, because the following record would revert back to him, and it would sell more if the Capitol record were successful. I wound up with both record companies throwing everything they had at my project. I felt like a girl with two suitors competing for my hand.

I was excited about finally getting to record Anna McGarrigle's "Heart Like a Wheel." I spent a lot of thought and energy planning the arrangement, masterfully written by violist David Campbell, and making sure that it included a cello solo. I particularly wanted the spare sound of a chamber group, rather than the more lush, orchestral approach that I thought had clogged up some of my previous releases. I had also figured out my guitar arrangement for "It Doesn't Matter Anymore" during my floor-waxing frenzy in the Beachwood apartment. Emmylou and I had worked up some harmonies to "I Can't Help It (If I'm Still In Love With You)," and she agreed to fly out and record it with me.

As I am primarily a ballad singer, I find it necessary to include uptempo songs on my records and in my performances so that the audience doesn't go to sleep listening to one slow song after another. As an afterthought, I decided to include on the record a song I'd been using to close our show. At the suggestion of Stone Poneys bandmate Kenny Edwards, I had learned it from the singing of soul singer Betty Everett, best known for her hit "The Shoop Shoop Song (It's in His Kiss)." It was called "You're No Good." We were tired of the arrangement we had been using onstage and decided to try something new. Ed Black, who played six-string guitar and pedal steel, started to play a rhythm riff on his Les Paul. Kenny Edwards had recently joined the band as the bass player, and he echoed the riff in octaves. Andrew Gold added a sparse drum part, giving me a basic track to sing over.

We did a few takes, picked one we liked, and then Andrew, who also played guitars and keyboards, went to work with Peter and began to build up layers of guitar, piano, and percussion tracks. After several hours of adding to the basic track, they started to compose and piece together Andrew's guitar solo. This was done by recording multiple tracks of Andrew playing the solo different ways and then editing together the bits they particularly liked. After that, they added more layers of Andrew playing guitars with different electronic effects until they had the solo completed. It took several more hours. When they had the solo assembled, we all sat down to listen to what had taken so long to put together, to see if it was as good as we thought it was. While they had been working, I had nicked out for an hour to eat dinner and brought a friend back with me. He made a comment about the solo, wondering why it suddenly sounded like the Beatles. Peter, who had worked so hard and was excited about how it had turned out, did not look happy. I asked to hear it again. Val Garay, our engineer, had been sitting at the console all day and into what was then the morning. He was tired. During the playback, he reached to turn on the track that contained the composite guitar solo, but he hit the wrong button and erased the entire thing. When he realized what he had done, his face turned as gray as putty. Peter was deadly calm. I could see the wheels turning in his head, frantically figuring out how to recapture what had been lost. Andrew opened his case, pulled out the guitar he had just packed up, and they started again. I went home and went to bed. I returned to the studio the next morning and heard the reconstructed solo. Peter, Val, and Andrew were exhausted. It sounded fabulous.

"You're No Good" was released as the single. We had included "I Can't Help It (If I'm Still In Love With You)," the duet I sang with Emmylou Harris, on the flip side. In February 1975 "You're No Good" went to number one on the Billboard Hot 100. In addition, "I Can't Help It (If I'm Still In Love With You)" went to number two on the country chart.

Number 38 Malibu Colony.

11

Malibu

HEART LIKE A WHEEL spawned two more hit singles, "When Will I Be Loved" and "It Doesn't Matter Anymore." Now I had enough money to buy a washing machine. I began to look for a house to go with it.

I had become an exercise fanatic and wanted to run in clean air and soft sand. I bought a small Cape Cod–style house at the beach in Malibu, about twenty minutes north of where I had lived in the Stone Poneys days in Santa Monica.

Canadian songwriter Adam Mitchell moved into the apartment over my garage. He was an ideal roommate. Adam wrote beautiful songs, was an excellent guitar player, and had a pure, falsetto-infused singing style that I loved, with the Celtic twang of his native Scotland. His family had emigrated from Scotland to Canada when he was still a boy. After getting his nose broken by a hockey stick, he took up the guitar and became a member of the Paupers, a successful Canadian rock band. He was also a runner. I was touring constantly, so having him live there meant that I had someone to look after my house while I was gone. Adam wanted quiet and solitude to work, and I had a piano that he could use whenever he needed it.

Emmylou introduced me to Nicolette Larson, who had been singing with Commander Cody and His Lost Planet Airmen, and we became friends immediately. Emmy and Nicolette had recorded a duet of a Carter Family song called "Hello Stranger," which had gotten a lot of airplay at Country Radio. Nicky had an earnest, midwestern prairie-girl sweetness and could make the dreariest chore fun. She had the most beautiful hair: thick and curly and falling past her waist. We traded clothes and luggage and deepest confidences about our romances. She would come out to the beach and spend days at a time. We baked cherry pies and whole wheat bread and sang harmonies with Adam.

John David Souther and Don Henley lived a little farther north of Malibu Colony and they would stop by occasionally and play their new songs. Sometimes they'd bring Jackson Browne or Glenn Frey, and it would be like our days on Camrose Place.

Neil Young asked me to sing harmonies on his *American Stars 'n Bars* album and came over to show me the songs. Nicolette was there that night, and he liked the way we sounded together, so we traveled to his beautiful ranch in Northern California and worked for several days. He called us the Saddle Bags.

I had first met Neil in 1971, the second time I performed on *The Johnny Cash Show*, which included Neil and also James Taylor. We taped the show at Nashville's Ryman Auditorium, legendary for being the original home of the Grand Ole Opry. On one of our nights off, I was invited by Earl Scruggs's teenage guitar wizard son, Randy, to a performance of the Opry and was introduced to Dolly Parton. I remember thinking that she had the most beautiful skin I had ever seen. She had an effervescent charm to go with it. I had heard her recording of a song she had written called "Jolene," and told her how much I admired it. I also admired the huge, fluffy skirt she wore, and she told me I shouldn't think she was a dumb country girl because of the way she was dressed. The idea hadn't occurred to me, but I took her at her word.

After working all day taping the Cash show, John Boylan and I went over to Quadrafonic Studios just south of Music

Row, where Neil was recording *Harvest*. Neil had asked James and me to sing backup harmonies on "Heart of Gold" and "Old Man." James also played a six-string banjo that was tuned like a guitar. They wanted us to sing on the same mike. This created a problem, as I am short and James is very tall. He wound up sitting on a chair to accommodate his banjo playing, while I knelt on the floor beside him, stretching to reach the mike and the ridiculously high notes that I had to sing to get a harmony above James. This went on hour after hour until morning with no complaints. When the music is good, you don't get bored and you don't get tired. "Heart of Gold," one of the songs we recorded that night, became the biggest single of Neil's career. We walked out of the studio into a freezing dawn and a record snowstorm. We found it delightful.

By the time we recorded *Stars 'n Bars*, several years later, Neil had a complete recording studio at his ranch. It included the old tube mixing board that had been removed from Hollywood's legendary Gold Star Recording Studios, where producer Phil Spector had recorded his "Wall of Sound" hits. As I had learned on the *Harvest* sessions, Neil was a bit of a reactionary in his recording style. Instead of recording a basic track and overdubbing for days, Neil liked to have everyone playing at once, giving his records a raw, spontaneous sound that was unmistakably his.

There is no one right way to record. It is a matter of personal style. When I recorded on *Graceland* with Paul Simon in the mid-1980s, he built his records a few tracks at a time, layering sound like the seventeenth-century Dutch painter Vermeer layered oil paint. Neil's work is more like a pen and ink drawing. They are both masters.

At my suggestion, Nicolette recorded a song of Neil's called "Lotta Love" and had her first hit as a solo artist. In gratitude, her producer, Ted Templeman, had a great sound system installed in my new Mercedes convertible. I cruised up and down Sunset Boulevard, from Pacific Coast Highway to Hollywood, blasting the Beach Boys and admiring the way the salt crystals hung in the air, reflecting a rosy glow. Life was good.

I started working out with a trainer named Max Sikinger. He was about five feet tall and incredibly wise about the mysteries of the human body. I learned that he was the person about whom Eden Ahbez wrote his beautiful song "Nature Boy," recorded by Nat "King" Cole in 1948, which I have always loved. The song's description of Max is starkly accurate.

Max had been born in Germany and told me that when he was five years old, toward the end of World War I, he was with his mother in a train station and bombs began to explode. He was never able to find his mother again ("A little shy, and sad of eye"). He was taken in by a gang of street kids, his short stature probably due to many years of near starvation in the rubble of postwar Germany. At around age fifteen, he lied about his age and got a job on a merchant ship that docked in New York. Max jumped ship and worked his way across the United States, winding up in Southern California. Along with musclemen like Jack LaLanne, Max Gold, and Steve Reeves, he became one of the original fitness advocates found on Muscle Beach, a stretch of sand south of the Santa Monica Pier. Max started training contestants for the Mr. Universe contests, and by the time I first connected with him in the mid-1970s, he was training movie stars and teaching them about raw diets, juice fasts, and weight lifting. Now gyms are full of women working out with weights, but in those days, Max's girls were the only ones. He taught me that a long hike was a better cure for depression than years of then-fashionable Freudian analysis or drugs, whether obtained by prescription or on the street.

I am severely allergic to alcohol and have never been able to tolerate it in any amount. I attempted to get drunk a few times by drinking tequila, my father's drink of choice. The result was a bright red face and several days of throwing up. I never got any buzz, just went immediately to the hangover. Cocaine sent me straight to the doctor with a bloody nose, which required cauterization. While I was there, my doctor cheerfully explained to me that cocaine causes the cilia in the ear canal to lie down, and many never get up again. This can cause permanent hearing loss. As I recognized that my ears were an important item in my musical toolbox, it was the end of my interest in cocaine.

Max had given me a strong body and a welcome alternative to the drugs and carousing lifestyle of the music business. This was a rich gift indeed.

I bought a dappled gray Arabian horse and tried to resurrect my childhood adventures, but threading my way through overdeveloped suburban Los Angeles was never the same as the wild freedom I had experienced with my childhood friend Dana and our ponies, Murphy and Little Paint, in the Arizona desert.

Nicolette came out to the beach one day with a new pair of roller skates. They were not like the in-line Rollerblades used now or the rickety metal ones I had as a child, which fitted to my saddle shoes with a key that hung on a ribbon around my neck. They were shoe skates with wide vinyl wheels that gave a surprisingly smooth ride. It was like having a Cadillac on each foot.

Nicky and I started skating on Venice Beach, which we liked because it was full of extreme Southern California characters. There were old Jewish lefties playing chess, whatever was left of the Beat Generation, Muscle Beach bodybuilders, and street performers. There were also slackers and stoners of every description lying around enjoying the warm sun and the great-looking girls in skimpy clothing. Skating liberated us from car culture. If we saw something we liked, we could stop and join in immediately without having to park. If we didn't like what we saw, we could roll on by.

The two of us were both novice skaters and could stop only by grabbing on to a pole or a tree. We had a pal named Dan Blackburn, who worked as a news correspondent for NBC. He was a good skater and offered to meet us at the beach and give us some tips. Dan said he would bring a friend he wanted us to meet.

He arrived at the designated hour and introduced us to a slender brunette, quiet and pretty, with a refined, well-brought-up manner. Her name was Leslie. We skated for an hour or so, until we were accosted by a tangle of people who were lying on the ground, trying to grab our ankles and begging for water. Some of them were eating dirt. They were obviously wasted on something strong. Somebody said it was "angel dust," which was the street name for PCP. The analgesic effect of angel dust can prevent users from realizing they need water, and by the time the drug starts to wear off, they are desperate with thirst.

We managed to slide away and skated to a nearby restaurant for lunch. After we ordered, we began to talk about how we felt sorry and embarrassed for the people we had seen, that they had been shorn of any dignity they may have possessed, and that angel dust looked like a bad drug. Nicky and I had never tried it and wondered what could be its appeal. Quiet Leslie became animated and said that yes, it was a very bad drug and could cause one to do things one would never do when sober. She said she knew this because she herself had done some bad things under the influence of drugs and had gone to jail. Remembering my own jail experience, I naively asked her what she was arrested for. "Murder," she replied.

"Well, who did you murder?" Nicky sputtered.

Leslie replied that her full name was Leslie Van Houten and that she had been part of Charles Manson's "family."

Nicolette and I were choking on our burgers. She seemed so nice and normal. We wondered as politely as we could how she had gotten out of jail and could be lunching and roller skating with us instead of sitting in a cell with the rest of her cohorts. She was out on an appeal because her attorney disappeared during the trial and so she was found to have had ineffective assistance at trial. As she saw it, the combination of Charles Manson's influence plus the drugs he had encouraged her to take would convince the court that she was not in her right mind and therefore innocent.

Dan and Leslie left us pondering how someone's life could change so irrevocably from normal to grotesquely tragic. As we skated back to where the car was parked, we wondered, could this happen to either of us? Or someone we loved? It definitely reinforced the hearing-loss argument against drugs. I remember feeling so disturbed and distracted that I lost track of what my feet were doing and fell hard on the concrete. This, added to my fall down the stairs at the Capitol Theatre a few years earlier, caused years of back problems. Leslie's appeal, no surprise, was ultimately unsuccessful, as she was retried and ultimately found guilty. After close to a year of freedom, she was returned to prison, where she remains to this day.

The phone was ringing in my Malibu cottage. It was Emmylou, saying that she had Dolly Parton sitting in her living room, and she wanted me to come over. Needing no more encouragement, I jumped in my car, pushed it as fast as I dared through the winding curves of Sunset Boulevard, and arrived at her house in Coldwater Canyon in record time.

Emmy and Dolly were sitting on the sofa, trading stories and laughing together. Emmy had her guitar out, and, very shortly, we began to play music. Dolly suggested a Carter Family jewel, "Bury Me Beneath the Willow," and we sang it in three-part harmony. All of us were surprised and stunned by the effect of our voices together. Emmy and I had played and sung together in lots of situations with lots of different people, including Neil Young, Roy Orbison, George Jones, and Ricky Skaggs. As we are all accomplished singers and players, it generally sounded pretty good. This new sound, however, was something different. We each seemed to realize it at the same time and immediately began to scratch around for other songs that we could sing together.

In American traditional music, there are lots of trio configurations for men but not so many for women. Bluegrass singing has been a man's domain, and rightly so. It is the attempt to push the male harmonies so high — a wail one notch below a scream — that gives the vocal blend an edge and a tension creating what is called the "high, lonesome sound."

Styles of harmonizing for women seem to me no less urgent and a great deal more reflective. Both men and women worked hard in the rural communities that gave us our rich treasury of Americana music. For men, it was the bone-crushing work of farming, mining, or building railroads and bridges. For women, it was seven days a week of laundering, cleaning, looking after children, and putting three meals on the table. When they did have some time to steal away and play music, I imagine them sitting in a tidy parlor, sharing their sorrows, joys, and disappointments with sisters or bosom friends. They would be playing whatever instruments and at whatever musical proficiency they were able to acquire; then they would scurry back to the unrelenting business of running a household.

The sound we were making wasn't bluegrass and it wasn't honky-tonk country music.

It wasn't even restricted to what Dolly referred to as "old-timey music," as we also wanted to explore more recently written material like the songs of Kate and Anna McGarrigle, or Linda Thompson, who was making remarkable records with her then husband, British musician Richard Thompson. We came to regard it as "parlor music"—something subtler and more genteel than bluegrass, honky-tonk, or the current pop music we heard on the radio.

We decided we would like to make a record together. While the merits of this idea seemed obvious to us, it was not immediately apparent to our respective managers or record companies.

There had been a number of attempts to forge and record "supergroups," which were composed of hugely successful and easily recognizable names from various rock bands. Sometimes the music from these groups turned out well, and sometimes not. We weren't trying to exploit the fact that we were three established names. We wanted to do it because at our deepest level of instinct, we suspected musical kinship.

Of course, trying to sort out the conflicts and demands of three different careers being represented by separate managers, agents, and record companies made singing together professionally almost impossible. We never did manage to align the planets for a concert tour, but we eventually carved enough time out of our schedules to make two albums over the years.

Musically, I found the experience very satisfying, with each of us bringing something different to the sound. Emmy usually found the best songs. Dolly's Appalachian style, with its beautiful ribbon-bow embellishments, lent an authenticity to the more traditional songs. Dolly and Emmy are both natural harmony singers, but the process of sorting out the more difficult harmony parts usually fell to me. We would try singing the songs in every vocal configuration, shifting around who sang high or low harmonies and who sang lead, and then choose what sounded best for that particular song. We also could duet successfully in any combination: Emmy and I, Dolly and I, or Dolly and Emmy. My favorite approach, which we used, for example, on "My Dear Companion," was for Emmy to start the lead, me to join her with a harmony underneath, and then have Dolly soaring above, dipping and gliding like a beautiful kite. I found I was able to sing with them in ways that I was not able to do by myself. I am seldom happy listening to my own recordings because I will hear something I think I should have done better, but the sound that the three of us made together seemed altogether different from our individual sounds and could be listened to with a rare sense of objectivity.

It was 1987 by the time we sorted out the logistics of synchronizing three busy careers and released *Trio.* Our earlier attempt to make a record when we first started trying to sing together in the mid-1970s was disappointing and never released. We each chose favorite tracks from those sessions and incorporated them into our individual projects. Still, we wanted very much to release an entire album of the three of us singing together. With Dolly between recording contracts, and Emmy and I each signed to labels that belonged to the Warner Bros. conglomerate, it seemed like an ideal time to resurrect the idea. We decided to have George Massenburg produce, as he had shown extraordinary sensitivity to the recording requirements of acoustic instruments when he worked with John Starling and the Seldom Scene. We called Starling right away and asked him to come out to play guitar. Emmy and I had great trust in John's musical sensibility, so we also asked him to help us shape our vision of what the trio should sound like.

As usual, Emmylou came in with an armload of beautiful songs. Mostly traditional in style, they also included the unlikely choice "To Know Him Is to Love Him," the Teddy Bears' 1958 classic written by Phil Spector. We recorded it with a band that we had assembled from the community of virtuoso acoustic string band instrumentalists that Emmy and I had long admired and played with. They included Mark O'Connor playing mandolin and guitarist Ry Cooder playing a seductively indolent, sleepwalking electric sound that only he can coax out of his equipment. We also had British guitarist Albert Lee and my cousin David Lindley. My old Stone Poneys bandmate Kenny Edwards played a Ferrington acoustic bass guitar. With Emmy's angelic, soaring lead, "To Know Him Is to Love Him" was a number one country hit for us. Emmy also suggested Linda Thompson's withering, sorrowful ballad "Telling Me Lies." It, too, succeeded as a single, and both songs won awards.

Dolly, Emmy, and I had a lot of fun recording together, and we even managed to squeeze a few television appearances and one later album into our three already overbooked schedules, but finding time to tour together was impossible, so we felt lucky to have such a musically satisfying experience and let the rest of it go.

In 1987, with artists like the Beastie Boys and Bon Jovi topping the charts, it was easy to understand why the record companies were scratching their heads trying to figure out how to sell such an eclectic stew. Dolly was no longer with her longtime label, RCA Records, so that left my company, Elektra/Asylum, and Emmy's company, Warner Bros., to figure out which one would release it. I suspect the negotiations more closely resembled a game of hot potato than it did a determined competition for a desired product. It was eventually decided that since Warner had a country division, it would take our record and construct an ad campaign aimed at the country music market.

To make matters more difficult, the marketing geniuses on the corporate side of the country music labels had decided to start using focus groups to test their products before they were developed or released. An example of this would be to ask the focus group whether they liked sad songs or happy songs. "We like happy songs!" the focus group would chirp, and the word would go back to the writers and producers to come up with "happy" songs to record. This made it especially hard on the songwriters, who rarely feel a need to write when they are happy, as then they are busy luxuriating in the pleasure of happiness. When something bad happens, they want to find a way to transcend it, so they write a song about it. When Hank Williams, one of the greatest and most successful country artists of all time, wrote a song like "Your Cheatin' Heart" or "I'm So Lonesome I Could Cry," he wasn't writing "happy" songs, yet they made the listener feel better. The listener could feel that someone else had gone through an experience similar to the listener's own, and then went to the trouble and effort to write it down accurately and share the experience like a compassionate friend might do. In this way, hearing a song like "I'm So Lonesome I Could Cry" could make the listener feel better, or "happy." Our record, with songs like the traditional "Rosewood Casket," which told a story of a dying and heartbroken sister's last request, didn't meet the focus group's requirements.

Jim Ed Norman, who had been the keyboard player in Shiloh, the band Don Henley played in before the Eagles, had very recently been made head of the Warner Bros. Records' country music division in Nashville. I suspect he had as little patience for the focus group approach to marketing music as we did. He seemed happy that the project had bounced into his lap and did his best to promote it.

When *Trio* was released, it went to number one on the country chart and remained there for five weeks. It rose to the Top Ten on the pop album chart and won a Grammy and an Academy of Country Music Award. It had four country hits, including the number one "To Know Him Is to Love Him." Within a year, it was certified platinum.

In the winter of 1979, the West Coast was hit with one ferocious rainstorm after another. The Pacific Coast Highway collapsed in a series of spectacular mudslides, making it impossible for me to drive home for weeks at a time. I found that I could take a long detour through Las Virgenes Canyon, but it also was subject to mudslides. This went on for three months, as the overburdened California Department of Transportation tried to fix a road that, due to inherent geological instability, never should have been built in the first place.

Trapped in Malibu, I watched the high waves strip the sand off the beach in front of my house, which was built with no foundation. Most of the houses in Malibu Colony have a glass-enclosed room, called a teahouse, which extends from the house proper out onto the beach. One night the waves were so high that they swept away the last of the sand from under my teahouse. With no support beneath, it splintered off the main house, my sofa cushions churning in the seawater as though they were in a giant washing machine. I realized I had broken the first rule of the desert: never buy a house in a flood plain.

I was keeping company with then-governor Jerry Brown, and he came out to look at the damage. By this time, the newspapers had begun to speculate on whether the governor was going to spend state money to protect his girlfriend's house. Precisely because of such speculation, Jerry had already decided not to, so I loaded my furniture and belongings into a moving van and sent them to storage, as I knew my house would surely collapse with the next surge of waves. Meanwhile, the other Malibu residents had heard that he wasn't going to spend money to protect the Colony because I lived there and felt they were being treated unfairly. After all, *they* weren't his girlfriend. I was expecting people to show up with torches and pitchforks, demanding his hide. Poor Jerry was being cornered in a situation he didn't cause and for which he couldn't offer a permanent solution.

Eventually, after Jerry talked at length to residents up and down the beach, the National Guard was called in to sandbag, and the houses were saved. I decided to look for a house in town, far from the recurring menace of the waves. I left Malibu believing that the California Coastal Commission was correct in insisting there be no new building on the beach, as the houses are too vulnerable, and development can disrupt the natural distribution of sand, resulting in precisely the situation I experienced. I also believe that the beach should not be owned as private property and the public should have unrestricted access to it.

I found a pretty house on Rockingham Drive in Brentwood that was designed by the architect Paul Williams, whose work I have long admired. It had a blue slate roof, lots of bedrooms for guests, and a pretty garden for my two Akita dogs to run. Adam's songwriting career had begun to heat up, and he moved to Santa Monica. Nicolette eventually moved into the Rockingham house with me. So did our pal Danny Ferrington, a luthier from rural Louisiana who built beautiful guitars entirely by hand. He made them at the behest of various musicians who sought him out to build their dream guitars. They included Johnny Cash, Keith Richards, George Harrison, Eric Clapton, Richard Thompson, and Ry Cooder, to name a very few. He would customize them by incorporating design suggestions from the musicians, accommodating both their visual and musical requirements. The guitars always sounded wonderful, with the acoustics tweaked for the particular playing style of the individual, whose technique and sound he knew in intimate detail. His brilliance lies in the fact that he can make the musician's wildest decorative fantasy seem tasteful. He made a tiny guitar for me that I could play while riding on our tour bus. Constructed of rosewood, ebony, spruce, abalone, and mother-of-pearl, it had a normal width neck and a small body for fitting in cramped spaces. The finished piece was elegant, even though I insisted the design elements include bunnies and tweeting birds. To each her own.

Sound check in London, Dan Dugmore playing guitar.

12

Getting Restless

MY LIFE HAD SETTLED into a fairly predictable routine. I'd make an album a year, which would take a few months to complete, and the rest of the time we would play one-night stands all over the country. By now my records were selling so well that instead of playing in intimate spaces like the Troubadour, I was being booked into hockey arenas and outdoor pavilions with huge audiences. The sound in those enormous places was kind of like being in a flushing toilet with the lid down. There was so much evil slapback ricocheting off the walls and ringing in the rafters, I'd swear I could still hear the lead guitar solo from the band that had played the week before. Those places were filled with zombie sound that simply refused to die; it just grew dimmer with time. In addition to that, people were milling about, passing joints, and drifting off in search of a hot dog or a cold beer at the concession stands that ringed the upper tiers.

Now, I was both delighted and deeply grateful that the records were selling and people were filling up those horrible-sounding arenas to hear me sing, but I couldn't help feeling that somehow both the audiences and the performers were getting a raw deal. The audience was getting a sound mix that was so distorted by the acoustics of the building that any delicate passages or musical subtleties were lost. This had a sinister effect on the way we created the music. Since they couldn't hear anything but loud, high-arching guitar parts and a cavernous backbeat, and because they didn't want to hold still for anything they hadn't heard on one of the albums, we began to tailor our recordings, consciously or not, to that big arena sound. This meant that all the really well-crafted and more delicate material, like "Heart Like a Wheel" or "Hasten Down the Wind," had to be slipped in between something that could survive the onstage acoustics.

I stubbornly hung on to those songs and layered them into the recordings like pills in hamburger. I knew that a melodic ballad was a better vehicle for my voice. It would allow me to mine a much richer emotional vein than what I could get from what I used to call a "short-note song." By that I meant a kind of uptempo song that a rock band would write to fit over a catchy riff, giving it something to do until the lead guitar player got to play his Big Solo. This kind of approach produced some excellent music from bands like Cream and the Rolling Stones, but even the musicians from those bands would regularly complain that they missed the musical heat of their club days and wished they could play in more musically sympathetic settings. Those boomy arenas hammered all the subtleties out of rock and roll as well and then proceeded to play midwife to the birth of heavy metal.

Since there are always talented players in these emerging categories, no matter how grating they may be to the ear of the more traditionally inclined, I was not surprised when the heavy metal band Metallica achieved a style that was huge and orchestral in its guitar textures, showing itself to be perfectly capable of producing beautiful melodies with unusual, finely constructed harmonies. My son at twelve was a devoted metal shredder, and once, while I was listening to him break down a Metallica song and then reconstruct it on the neck of his own guitar, I mentioned that I thought their stadium-size guitar textures resembled a symphony orchestra. He gave me a look of withering teenage scorn. I was vindicated when Metallica brought out

THE CLUB FILARMÓNICO TUCSONENSE in the 1890s.
My grandfather was the conductor. He can be seen fourth from the right
in the first row that is seated in chairs. He is holding his flute.

MY AUNT LUISA Espinel Ronstadt in the early 1920s.
Lansing Brown

MY PARENTS' engagement portrait.
Lansing Brown

IN OUR BACKYARD, age eleven.
Dana O'Sullivan

MY MATERNAL GRANDFATHER
Lloyd G. Copeman, with a baby
raccoon that he rescued and raised.

WITH BOBBY KIMMEL
in front of our house on
Hart Street, 1966.
Henry Diltz

EIGHTH GRADE wearing my Catholic school uniform.

AGE SIXTEEN wearing the dress my friend Liisa Wilska and my mother made for me.

SUZY, PETER, AND ME recording at Copper State Recording Studios as the New Union Ramblers in Tucson, 1964.

DISCUSSING "DIFFERENT DRUM" with arranger Jimmy Bond.
Henry Diltz

WITH NIK VENET listening to playback of "Different Drum." I wasn't sure about the arrangement. Nik was, and he won.
Henry Diltz

RIDING MY ARABIAN gelding, Blue, in the sub-urbanized "countryside" of Malibu.
Marilyn Meadows

PLAYING AT THE PALOMINO CLUB in Los Angeles, 1972. (left to right) Ed Black, Mike Bowden hidden behind me playing the bass, me, Mickey McGee (drums), Richard Bowden, Gib Guilbeau, and Herb Pedersen. In addition to Ricky Skaggs, Herb taught me a lot about bluegrass harmonies.

IN MY BETSEY JOHNSON singing dress that I wore for years. I always carried it wadded up in my purse in case the airlines lost our luggage.
Henry Diltz

BACKSTAGE at the Bitter End in New York with fiddle player Gib Guilbeau, 1970.

SINGING "PRISONER IN DISGUISE" with John David Souther at the Universal Amphitheater in L.A. *Henry Diltz*

THESE DAYS PERFORMING ARTISTS seem to have teams of stylists, makeup artists, hairdressers, and image-makers to create a look to present to the public. In those early years we never had anything like that, plus we didn't have any money. We wore mostly jeans or cut-offs with some kind of top. My mother was no longer sewing for me and I was absolutely clueless about what to wear. Nicolette Larson and I shopped at a place in downtown L.A. that had old lace and antique clothes. That was before they were called "vintage." After I had a few hits, I decided to have some clothes made, but I always lost weight during tours so by the time we worked our way to the East Coast they were falling off and looked terrible. I ran into Nicolette in New York and we decided to go look for something we could wear onstage. We went to a surplus store in Greenwich Village recommended by one of the guys in the band. They had a lot of little boy's clothes that were the perfect size for the little bodies Nicky and I had then. We each bought Cub Scout uniforms and some great old rayon Hawaiian shirts. I also bought some soccer shorts and some boxing shorts. That became my wardrobe for the tour. We played mostly outdoor pavilions that summer, and it would be hot and sweaty under the lights. By late August, the northern venues like Michigan and Minnesota were really cold after sundown. The Cub Scout suit was ideal because I could layer it with long underwear and add the hat and neckerchief for warmth. Perfect outdoor attire. *Henry Diltz*

DOLLY PARTON AND ME SITTING IN WITH EMMYLOU HARRIS at the Universal Amphitheater.

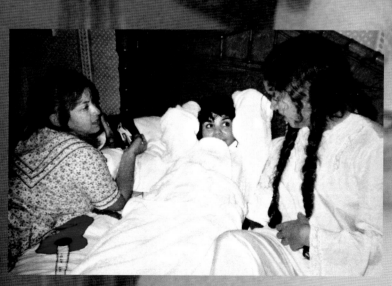

JENNY SHORE, ME, AND NICOLETTE LARSON hanging out in Danny Ferrington's room at my house on Rockingham Drive. Danny's mother made the guitar quilt for his bed. *Danny Ferrington*

RUNNING WITH JERRY on the beach in Malibu between the storms that washed away part of my house, 1978.

ME, DOLLY, AND EMMYLOU swinging on the back porch at Dolly's house in Tennessee.

FALLING HARD FOR KERMIT.

KENNY EDWARDS, ME, AND DANNY FERRINGTON holding the guitar that Danny made for Kenny.

WITH JOHN DAVID SOUTHER during the California Live tour in Japan, 1981.

WITH MY FATHER backstage at the Tucson Mariachi Conference.

PLÁCIDO DOMINGO, ME, AND JOE PAPP the night in 1984 when Plácido came to the Public Theater in New York to hear our production of La Bohème. *Martha Swope*

BACKSTAGE WITH THE STEP SISTERS on the *What's New* tour that I did with Nelson Riddle. (left to right) Liza, Elizabeth, me, and Rita. *J. Roy Helland*

REX SMITH, ME, AND KEVIN KLINE in *The Pirates of Penzance*, 1980. *Martha Swope*

SINGING THE ROLE OF MIMI in *La Bohème*
at the New York Public Theater.
Gary Morris sings Rodolfo.
Martha Swope

WITH NICOLETTE LARSON trying to get her new single on the radio.

WITH LONGTIME FRIEND and collaborator John Boylan in Egypt, 1983.

DURING REHEARSALS for *La Bohème.*

WITH ART DIRECTOR Kosh while shooting the album cover photo for *Cry Like a Rainstorm, Howl Like the Wind.* Kosh designed twenty albums for me, of which three won him Grammys for best album cover design. *Robert Blakeman*

MUSCLE SHOALS John Boylan producing.

an album it made with the San Francisco Symphony under the direction of Michael Tilson Thomas. All this is a long way to demonstrate that musicians reach for a rich acoustical setting like a plant reaches for light, and I was no exception.

Something else that made me sad about the action shifting out of the clubs and into the arenas was the fact that artists didn't get to see one another perform as much as when the folk rock music scene was centered on L.A.'s Troubadour or New York's Bitter End. The limited space of the Troubadour put the bathrooms in a back-hall area off the performance space. That meant everyone from the bar had to travel through the room where the stage was in order to visit the plumbing. Even if you were an up-and-coming hopeful hanging out in the bar but too broke to pay the admission fee, you could get a rich sampling of what was happening on the stage every time nature insisted. If you had been hired in the past by owner Doug Weston to play at the Troubadour, you got free admission, so when somebody interesting was playing, we veterans would crowd the staircase and the upstairs balcony night after night to see our favorites. I remember seeing artists like Joni Mitchell, James Taylor, the Flying Burrito Brothers, George Carlin, and Steve Martin play every night of a two-week engagement, two shows a night, and three on Friday and Saturday nights. This way, artists got to see a wider arc of another artist's talent, and some vigorous cross-pollination of musical styles was the happy result.

Seeing each other's shows in arenas didn't happen so naturally. The tickets were way more expensive, which left out the newbies, there was no place to hang out and mix socially, like the Troubadour bar—unless one had rare and privileged access backstage—and parking was a hassle. And then there was lousy sound, so we couldn't listen and dissect the music like we had been able to do in the smaller settings. In short, it became less likely for the artists to trip over the influence and inspiration of one another than it had been before.

I felt some stagnation setting in, and the relentless touring and endless repetition of the same songs over and over again promoted a creeping awareness that my music had begun to sound like my washing machine.

A promotional tour that took us to Great Britain, Germany, and France in the late 1970s jolted us back into the forgotten reality of what it was like to play in smaller, dedicated music venues. I was not particularly well known in Europe, so we were playing in medium-size theaters with proscenium stages and lots of chubby-faced cherubs in bas-relief cavorting around the walls. The cherubs and other fussy design elements, in addition to delighting my Victorian sensibility, softened the parallel surfaces of the theater walls and sweetened the sound. Finally, the dream I held so dear as a child had materialized: I was singing on a real stage in a real theater with a curtain. I was inspired.

The inspiration was short lived. We were soon back in the USA, pounding the same old circuit in the same distinctly uninspiring arenas. Add to this the gnawing loneliness of life lived perpetually in motion, with not enough time in any one place to nurture relationships or build trust. I was beginning to feel miserable. And trapped.

One night we were playing in Atlanta. We had spent the afternoon fooling around in the little shops that had been established in what is called Underground Atlanta, the recently excavated, fire-charred remains of the pre–Civil War city. Big, smudgy, black-ringed eyes were in style then, and I found what seemed like a particularly exotic way to achieve it in one of the little shops. It was an ancient cosmetic called kohl—new to my experience—which was some kind of black mineral ground into a fine powder, and recently shipped in from India. There was also a blue one, which was a departure for me, but I figured if I couldn't change my life so easily, I could at least change the color of my eye makeup, so I bought that too. It was packaged in a little clay pot with a pointed wooden stick screwed into the lid to use as an applicator.

I was hot to try it out and went immediately to the dressing room of the place we were playing (another arena) and started to smear the stuff around my eyes. The applicator stick and powdered medium were unfamiliar and clumsy for me to use, and I had accidentally dotted my cheeks with what looked like the blue measles. I finished the job of cleaning off all the little stray blue blobs and wondered what I was going to do for the forty-five minutes until I had to sing. I had finished the book I kept in my purse and was scowling at the concrete floor — wishing we were still in a European theater with cherubs and that I didn't have to face an all-night drive in the bus after the show — when someone knocked on the door, bringing me out of my little sulk. It was one of the security guards, who handed me a book that someone had sent backstage with a note attached saying that it was something he or she thought I might like. "Oh goody!" I thought. "Now I won't have to be bored."

I looked at the cover: *The Vagabond*, by Colette. "Never heard of this book," I thought. Never heard of Colette, either. She had just one name. Like Cher.

I opened the book and began to read. The story is set in France in 1910. La Belle Époque! My favorite era! There is a woman about my age who performs in music halls sitting backstage in her dressing room. She is applying blue greasepaint circles around her eyes, and some of it has run down her face. Blue for her too? She also uses kohl. Kohl again! I just heard of the stuff that afternoon.

What else? She is kind of bored. She has already read the book she has with her. She is waiting to go onstage and do her act. She has lost the inspiration to continue in her career as "a woman of letters" and is trying to establish herself as "a woman on the stage." Things are not going as well as they could, and she knows that she is "in for a bad fit of the blues." She is thinking about her dog and her kind-of-awkward boyfriend whom she misses somewhat. There is a knock on her door . . .

I have a beloved Akita dog and an awkward boyfriend somewhere. I feel that I'm "in for a bad fit of the blues." I can relate!

I finished the book that night on the long bus ride. I started to ponder: How can I work in a more theatrical setting, in smaller theaters, and not a different place every night?

13

Meeting Joe Papp

Photo by Martha Swope.

With Joe Papp backstage at
the New York Public Theater
during La Bohème.

I PICKED UP THE next available phone and called my pal John
Rockwell in New York to whine about my predicament. John
wrote about music for *The New York Times* for more than thirty
years and is one of the rare critics who can write with equal authority about both classical music and contemporary pop music.
We met in 1973, when he came to my apartment on Beachwood
Drive in the Hollywood Hills to interview me. He noticed that I
had a book on my shelf called *Before the Deluge: A Portrait of Berlin
in the 1920s,* by Otto Friedrich. (Yes, I lent the book to Jackson
Browne, who wrote a good song with the same title. This is done
frequently and is legal. *The Moon Is a Harsh Mistress,* the title of
a 1966 science-fiction novel by Robert Heinlein, comes imme-

diately to mind. The great songwriter Jimmy Webb loved the title and appropriated it for a song that I later sang on my album *Get Closer*.) *Before the Deluge* was about the Weimar Republic in Germany, just as Hitler was coming to power, and all the missed opportunities that might have stopped him. I had become fascinated with the tragedy of this era, as well as the glamour of prewar Berlin, the architectural innovation, the declining importance of virgin brides (no dowries in a bad economy), the gender-bending clothing styles, the hair and makeup styles, and the wonderful music (Kurt Weill, the Comedian Harmonists). David Bowie was beginning to experiment with one exotic image after another, and in the mid-1970s his look seemed eerily similar to that earlier time. I wondered then if we were heading into our own little version of the Weimar Republic here in the United States, to be followed by the harsh realities of fascism and aggressive imperialism.

Rockwell, who lived in Germany as a child, earned his PhD in German cultural history, and wrote his thesis on the Weimar Republic, is a fountain of information, and we bonded. The day I called him to complain so bitterly about my stagnant state of mind and need for angels in the architecture of my place of employment, he suggested that the next time I came to New York, he would like to take me to meet a fellow named Joe Papp. "Who is Joe Papp?" I asked. Joe Papp, intoned Rockwell, was a brilliant theater man who had revolutionized the interpretation of Shakespeare by insisting it be made accessible across cultural, economic, and social lines, using racially diverse casts and presenting it to the public at the Delacorte Theater in Central Park for free. He also was not afraid to bring in people from other areas of show business. Maybe he had some ideas about what to do with me.

The next time I found myself in New York, Rockwell found a hole in his very busy schedule that corresponded to a hole in Joe Papp's even busier schedule and took me in a taxi to the New York Public Theater in Lower Manhattan. I still was not very knowledgeable about Papp, and had no idea that he had helped launch a staggering number of fabulous careers, including those of George C. Scott, Meryl Streep, James Earl Jones, Martin Sheen, and Wallace Shawn, and shows such as *Hair* and *A Chorus Line*.

Joe Papp was brilliant and compelling. I don't say this lightly. I could count on one hand the number of men I have met who exuded his magnetism and competence. There was also his thoughtful, curious, and boundlessly informed intelligence, which could have the effect of a wild tiger at the end of a frayed leash. He listened very politely to my lunatic raving about Colette and wanting to sing on a stage with a curtain, and then went about the rest of his day meeting with the long line of people of infinitely greater ability and importance than me. I doubt that he gave our meeting a second thought.

In 1979 the city cut Papp's funding for presenting Shakespeare in Central Park that summer—something he had been doing since 1962—and he was angry about it. He decided he wouldn't do Shakespeare that summer. Instead, he would put on Gilbert and Sullivan's operetta *The Mikado*. He asked the acclaimed director and playwright Wilford Leach to direct it, but Leach didn't like Gilbert and Sullivan and said he didn't think he wanted to do it. But, since Papp was very keen on the idea, Leach went to a record store to buy a copy of *The Mikado* and, for some reason, came home instead with a copy of *The Pirates of Penzance*. This he decided he *did* like, but he thought that the traditional way of performing it was too stiff. Leach wanted to approach it like a brand-new play. Since Gilbert and Sullivan was the pop music of its time, he decided he wanted to use contemporary pop singers from our time.

Leach liked to watch the *Today* show when he woke up in the morning. Coincidentally, John Rockwell had a monthly slot on the program, talking about music. While Leach was in the process of casting *Pirates*, he saw Rockwell on *Today*, talking about me.

Leach liked my voice and decided that I was the person he wanted to cast in the role of Mabel, the soprano ingénue. He went into Papp's office to tell him his idea, and Papp said, "I've met her; she wants to work here." He asked his assistant to call me at home in Malibu.

The call came while I was upstairs taking a shower. Jerry Brown was sitting downstairs next to the phone, so he answered it. Jerry had seen *H.M.S. Pinafore* when he was in school, and that was what he remembered of Gilbert and Sullivan, so when I came downstairs, he told me that someone named Joe Papp had called and he wanted me to sing in *Pinafore*. I was delighted! During the time that my sister had sung the alto role of Buttercup all those years ago when I was six, I had learned the soprano part of Josephine out of the big book of Gilbert and Sullivan that sat on our piano at home, and I loved her songs. I burst into a chorus of "Refrain Audacious Tar" and then started to sing the little heartbroken ballad "Sorry Her Lot." This one was my favorite, and I couldn't believe I might have a chance to sing it!

I picked up the phone and called Joe Papp immediately. I told him I would love to sing *Pinafore*. I was a little disappointed when he said that it was *Pirates*, because I had never learned those songs, and I wasn't sure that I would like them as much. He assured me that *Pirates* had a wealth of lovely songs for Mabel to sing, and if I wanted the part, it was mine. I then insisted that I should fly back to New York and audition for them, since I wanted to be sure that he and the director would be happy with the way I would sing it. I didn't want any unpleasant surprises.

During the flight to New York, I was fretting about my appearance. I was growing my hair out from the really short cut that I'd worn on the cover of *Mad Love*, my most recent record, and the back of my hair was streaked with big chunks of cyclamen pink. It was the beginning of the eighties, and we were just starting to experiment with the wildly unnatural hair colors that I remember first seeing in their most prescient splendor in Stanley Kubrick's *A Clockwork Orange*. I made the mistake of combining the extreme color process with a permanent to make my straight hair curly like Nicolette's, and my hair simply broke off. The stringy bits that were left made me look like a Polish Crested chicken. I cut them off with my sewing scissors, leaving a mess that my regular hairdresser was unable to repair.

Many actress friends had told me that when they read for a part, they dressed up to resemble the character they were trying to portray. *The Pirates of Penzance* was set in Victorian times. I collected antique clothes and had some very pretty white lace Victorian summer frocks in my closet, but it was early spring and too cold in New York to wear them, so I walked into one of the rehearsal halls at the Public Theater in cowboy boots, jeans, sweater, and short pink hair. I didn't look very Victorian. Joe Papp was there and introduced me to Wilford Leach and music director Bill Elliott. I liked them both immediately, and that never changed.

I still had never seen a score or heard a recording of *Pi-*

rates, which they advised was unnecessary until they decided whether to perform the pieces in the original keys or to shift to other keys to accommodate the pop singers. I didn't like the idea of changing keys, as it can make the sound of the orchestra murky at the very least, but I decided to keep mum until we explored it. We started at the piano, and I asked Bill to show me the highest notes written for Mabel in the score. He played me a D above high C. I was singing the high C in concerts with my band night after night, so I didn't think the D—one note up the scale—would be a problem. In the show, I wound up singing Mabel's "Poor Wandering One" in two keys: the original one, plus a lower key to insert a more contemporary flavor into the interpretation. I had a really high voice with an upper extension that I never got a chance to use much in rock and country except for some little flourishes and embellishments, so it wasn't as strong as the register where I had been belting "Heat Wave" and "Blue Bayou" all those years. This was going to cause me some trouble, but I didn't know it yet. Also, Bill wrote me a cadenza (a short ornamental solo passage) to sing in the first act and again at the end of the show that went up to a very high E flat in the nosebleed octave, just like Violetta in *La Traviata*. With eight shows a week, that would add up to sixteen E flats—something that frail, consumptive Violetta would never dream of attempting in real opera. But I didn't know that yet either.

I returned home and repacked my suitcase for a trip to London. I had been invited to perform on TV's *The Muppet Show* and decided to invite my parents along for fun, thinking that they could see the sights in London while I rehearsed with Kermit, Miss Piggy, and the rest of the effervescent Muppets cast.

By now I had the score for *Pirates* wedged carefully between layers of pajamas and the vintage Victorian clothes I planned to wear on the show. I had also transferred the vinyl disc recording to a cassette tape and loaded it into my new pink Sony Walkman, which was the hot portable sound innovation of the time.

We stayed at the Savoy Hotel, which, coincidently, is next to the Savoy Theatre, where the D'Oyly Carte players performed all of Gilbert and Sullivan's revered operettas in the time of Queen Victoria. I have always loved this hotel for its Victorian design remodeled in the 1930s in the Art Deco style. The suites we stayed in had high ceilings, pretty moldings, coal fireplaces, and buttons you could press to summon the room service waiter. He would appear anytime of the night or day, take the order, and return promptly with a tea cart loaded with steaming pots of freshly brewed loose tea, delicate little tea sandwiches, and hot scones with jam and clotted cream. Yum! There was also a button to summon the maid next to the sumptuously deep bathtub in case one had difficulty reaching the soap. I never used that button, but I loved soaking neck deep in the hot water, taking in all the vintage details of the curved doors, thirties hardware, and freestanding sinks, much of which I copied in a house I remodeled in San Francisco years later. Our rooms had a sweeping view of the river Thames, and the night after my first rehearsal with the Muppets, I dug the new score out of my suitcase and put on my Walkman headphones. While listening to the beautiful duet "Ah, Leave Me Not to Pine," I could see Big Ben towering serenely in the moonlight. I was hearing the music for the first time in that setting, the very one into which it had been born.

Jim Henson and Frank Oz, the original creators of the Muppets, were tremendous fun to work with. The first time I had ever seen them work was at the 1979 Grammys. I had come in when the Muppets were still rehearsing, so I was able to watch them from the back and could see the contortionist poses that Henson and Oz had to assume in order to get the puppets to move right for the cameras. They could watch the way the puppets looked from the camera's viewpoint by looking at small video monitors. I was completely fascinated and impressed by their artistry and have remained a reverent fan of puppetry ever since.

I was excited about getting to work with them and had an idea that I wanted to have a romance with Kermit. I suggested a song, the Gershwins' "I've Got a Crush on You," which I could sing in a confessional manner to him, and then a rock-and-roll song, "The Shoop Shoop Song (It's in His Kiss)," for after he kissed me. (I was warned severely not to let my lipstick touch his green felt lips, or it would stain, and the Creature Shop would have to construct a new body.) Since Kermit had already made a serious commitment to Miss Piggy, our affair was doomed, and we had to part like Humphrey Bogart and Ingrid Bergman in the last scene of *Casablanca*. In a wave of sympathy, the entire Muppets ensemble, including a surprisingly forgiving Piggy, joined Kermit and me in a finale of "When I Grow Too Old to Dream," a 1930s standard that I'd recorded on my album *Living in the USA*. Somewhere in the middle, I sang "Blue Bayou" in the aforementioned Victorian togs and bare feet, with a chorus of frogs chirping along from lily pads floating in an artificial bayou. The set was built to resemble Disneyland's Blue Bayou restaurant at the entrance to the Pirates of the Caribbean attraction. It was ridiculously good fun.

I sometimes wonder what a scientist like Oliver Sacks might discover about how the human brain can compartmentalize if he had watched our rehearsals. During breaks, the puppeteers would sit chatting, speaking as themselves and also chiming in fully in the persona of the one or more puppet characters they had just been operating. Sometimes the puppets would squabble among themselves, or Miss Piggy would make sarcastic remarks to her operator, Frank Oz, about the script as he was writing it. The effect was a delightful and wonderfully creative bedlam, with people strolling casually into and out of reality for hours at a time and getting paid to do so.

Years later, Kermit and I reunited briefly (much too briefly for my liking) to sing a duet of "All I Have to Do Is Dream" on a Muppets record. After that, he returned to his love nest with that pig, and I never saw him again.

Singing the role of Mabel in The Pirates of Penzance.

14

The Pirates of Penzance

I RETURNED FROM MY *Muppet Show* experience to the new house I had bought on Rockingham, which had barely any furniture in it, and started to get ready to move to New York for the summer. I had found an apartment on Manhattan's Upper West Side, and was wondering what life would be like in the truly urban, densely packed, and wildly stimulating environment of New York City.

Peter Asher, my manager, thought it was a great idea for me to do *Pirates*, although he was understandably concerned that it would disrupt the safe routine of an album and several tours a year, and might have a negative effect on the momentum he'd been able to build into my career.

Drawing on his own theater experience, he tried his best to give me a crash course in theater etiquette and protocol so that I wouldn't offend the others through simple ignorance. The most important thing, I gathered, was to never be late. Being late is a tremendous imposition on cast and crew, who don't enjoy twiddling their thumbs while waiting for a self-absorbed, unprofessional rock star, and can run up the bill in a budget that is already stretched taut. It is guaranteed to create resentment.

The first day of rehearsal, I was careful to leave in what I thought was plenty of time to get a cab and make it all the way from West Seventy-First Street to the Public Theater in Greenwich Village. The whole island wasn't that big, so how long could it take? But the cabbie realized that his passenger in the backseat didn't know the city, and he took an extralong route. I was fifteen or twenty minutes late when I finally arrived—completely embarrassed. It earned me a serious scolding from our stage manager and didn't happen a second time.

Just before I met Rex Smith, who had been cast to play opposite me in the part of Frederic, I was introduced to a life-size cutout photograph of Rex clothed in little more than his considerable male pulchritude. It had somehow appeared near the door of the rehearsal room. I suspect Rex was writhing, but he didn't crack. He was so handsome that I was inwardly groaning and hoping he wasn't loaded with glamour-boy attitude. He wasn't. He was eager and exuberant, a little naive, extremely candid, and had great instincts. I decided to like him.

A rehearsal room is a volatile space. It generally contains little more than the appropriate number of chairs and the talent that people bring with them. If their talent is compatible and synergistic and a clear idea emerges, the work will feel effort-less. With great luck, it can become ecstatic.

Sometimes, no matter how carefully selected the cast or mu-sicians, how brilliant the writer or director, it can become less than the sum of the parts. At this point, the work becomes mor-bidly effortful. Anguish descends like a leaden slime, and the par-ticipants can't wait to be finished and out of that room. It is hard to overstate just how embarrassing and miserable this feels, even when no one is particularly to blame. I am not religious, but a rehearsal room can seem like a hallowed space; a place for trans-formation. A performer enters it at his peril. Rex understood this. As we were walking into the rehearsal room at Joe Papp's Public Theater, he took my hand, his eyes wide with anticipation and excitement. "This is like going into church," he said.

The first thing we did at rehearsal after introducing our-selves and the characters we were playing was to sit down and sing the whole show through, from beginning to end. This was thrilling, as there are several standout choral pieces, and we got to hear how the vocal ensemble — with its more natural approach to singing the Victorian melodies — was going to work. Wilford and Bill decided to add another song for me to sing and asked if I could suggest something from another Gilbert and Sullivan show. I could! "'Sorry Her Lot'!" I shrieked. "It's from *Pinafore*! I already know it!" I sang it for them. It was a perfect fit for the spot they had in mind. I was delighted to get to sing the song I had loved since childhood. I couldn't wait to tell my sister.

The next few days found us on our feet and "off book," with a chance to see what moves choreographer Graciela Daniele had cooked up. Tony Azito, who played the constable, got up and did a wonderfully rubber-jointed dance to accompany his lament to constabulary duties. His reedy voice had echoes of Berlin cabaret mixed with the asceticism of monastic chant. I was breathless.

Kevin Kline began to demonstrate some hilarious physical schtick he had worked out to make his character seem dashing, bold, and hopelessly confused all at once: Errol Flynn with a touch of dementia. I can see fragments of Kevin's Pirate King layered into the send-up of Keith Richards in Johnny Depp's Captain Jack Sparrow, the character he created for the movie *Pirates of the Caribbean*.

Rex was rightfully in Kevin's thrall, so his character followed the Pirate King around the stage like an eager puppy dog. This set up a most charming dynamic between the two male heartthrobs, and they never had to compete with each other.

Our Major-General Stanley was George Rose. British born and a seasoned theater professional to the tenth power, he humbled us all with his lightning-speed patter songs. These had been prepared to a perfection I wouldn't have thought possible well before rehearsals ever started. He was dazzling.

Patricia Routledge, another immaculately skilled product of

the British musical theater, sang and acted Nurse Ruth's batty Victorian songs and manner with great naturalness and seamless comedic skill. I overheard her say something to Kevin one day when they were rehearsing a scene, she being the seasoned pro and he the new rising star. She said, "Kevin, what do you think we are trying to do with this scene?" Kevin answered, "To make it funny?"

"No," she replied in a somewhat severe tone. "We don't need to make it funny. We need to make it clear. If it is clear, *then* it will be funny." I thought this was brilliant advice, and so did Kevin. I try to apply it to everything I sing. For instance, if one is singing a sad song, it is better to tell the story as clearly and simply—even as journalistically—as one can. It will have a stronger effect on the listener and seem more emotional than a teary, overwrought delivery.

Finally, the female chorus of Mabel's giddy sisters emerged as an amalgamated star in its own right. Wonderful comedy bits and singing that traced a bipolar flip from angelic sweetness to brassy belting erupted from them on a nightly basis.

With a cast as strongly professional and charming as this one, I figured the show would run like a locomotive, and as long as I didn't fall down on the stage, I would be carried along by sheer momentum. Because my lines were all sung, I hadn't quite realized that I was acting and my performance still needed some fleshing out in order for Mabel's character to emerge.

Wilford was the kind of director who left his actors alone to do their work, but I didn't know anything about acting and was feeling rudderless. One day we were rehearsing outside in the full sun at the Delacorte Theater in Central Park, where we would open soon. The combination of that summer's record-breaking temperatures and brutal humidity left me yearning for the relative comfort of the dry heat in Arizona. Keith David, Juilliard trained in acting and one of the strongest pirate voices, asked me what I thought was uppermost in Mabel's mind. "A sno-cone!" I responded desperately. Keith was thoughtful. Then he said to me, "Mabel wants Frederic. There is no heat in her world. Only Frederic." I looked over at my big black Akita dog, Molly, who was panting in the shade at the side of the stage. Molly and I had been in the park for about a week, and she had become very interested in the squirrels. When she saw one, she developed an intense concentration that saturated and molded her whole body. She pricked her ears and cocked her head and surrendered her entire fuzzy self to one impulse. I decided to use that. I morphed myself into a canine soprano, and Mabel was born. When Robin Boudreau, one of the girls in the chorus, remarked to me one day that pets and their owners often resembled each other, I knew I was there.

Mabel was also somewhat pigeon-toed, while I am more duck-footed. The cooler side of Mabel's nature must have been alarmed at the desperate, hurtling motion in Frederic's direction, so her feet kept trying to turn around and run the other way. An odd little collection of quirks and impulses like these began to sprout and grow in me, in what I imagine was the most rudimentary beginning of the craft of acting. Rudimentary was as far as I ever got, but it was enough to carry me around the stage for the entire year that I stayed with the show. *Pirates* opened on July 15, 1980. It was my birthday.

People routinely describe the Public Theater summer productions in Central Park as magical, and though this may seem a well-worn expression, it is quite accurate. Shape shifting and transcending mundane states are regularly associated with the concept of magic, and with good theater, that is precisely what you get. For me, there was an added element of time travel. Night after night, I waited to go on at the side of the stage in my Victorian bonnet and white summer frock, a soft breeze ruffling my skirt, the moon sailing sweetly overhead. Beyond me was a large pond that made a lovely natural extension to our painted sea. On the opposite shore was a weather station housed in Belvedere Castle, a Gothic-style observation tower built in 1867. Just beyond the tree line was the still-intact Art Deco silhouette of the Manhattan skyline of the 1930s. It sometimes felt like Fred Astaire himself could have burst out of that skyline with his top hat and cane and tap-danced on the moon.

Living in such a tightly packed environment, the chances to savor nature's nocturnal delights are limited mostly to ball games and trips to Coney Island beach. A baseball fan might vehemently disagree with me, but I think these experiences would shrivel next to an evening in Joe Papp's magic theater in the great outdoors of Central Park.

It had its drawbacks. We were terrorized by lightning, pummeled by wind, and soaked with rain that turned our costumes into Saran Wrap. Then there were the bugs. While singing, we swallowed them nightly, but once, just before the kissing scene I had with Rex at the end of the second act, a huge mosquito got trapped in the gluey layer of my lip gloss. I could feel it struggling to free itself, and when Rex leaned in to kiss me, his eyes were bulging out of his head. He was struggling to keep his composure, and so was I. After our kiss, Rex got to leave the stage, but I had to stay and sing "Sorry Her Lot" from beginning to end with a giant mosquito playing its death scene to the very last row on my lower lip.

One night Papp showed up at my dressing room door with Mayor Ed Koch in tow. Looking back, I am sure that Joe brought him down to see our very successful show and meet the cast in an attempt to get back his funding. At the time, I wasn't aware of any of these political subplots, but I recognized the photographer he had with him: a particularly aggressive paparazzo who had stationed himself at the Eighty-Second Street entrance to the park. No cars were allowed in that area, so daily I was on foot and at his mercy while he swooped and darted at me, calling me the b-word, the c-word—any foul thing he could think of to get an emotional reaction and wind up with a more interesting picture to sell. Richard, my bodyguard, would remind me out of the corner of his mouth that his job was to keep me from hitting the photographer with a rock because of the lawsuit it would surely bring. I behaved.

But when I saw the smugly triumphant expression on the photographer's face as he stood behind Papp and Mayor Koch shooting pictures of me in my bathrobe and pin curls, my face streaked with cold cream, I didn't behave. My nature being somewhat phlegmatic, I don't have a particularly short temper. In fact, my temper has a very long fuse. The only trouble is that when it finally ignites, it is connected to an ice-covered volcano. While the volcano was issuing a pyroclastic flow of frenzied activity at the photographer, the icy part of me was calmly and logically explaining to Joe that the fellow had been tormenting me for a couple of weeks, that I didn't think it was fair, and that I was going to strangle him with his camera strap and then smash the hated camera on the concrete floor, causing the film to roll out and render the photos useless. I believe I was successful in these efforts, as the photos never appeared. I then walked calmly to the showers at the end of the hall to wash off the rest of the makeup and cold cream, and the sticky humidity of the summer night. When I came back, Joe was still standing in the hallway with the somewhat stunned mayor, explaining to him how important it was for actresses to have temperament.

Because of our surprising success in Central Park, Joe Papp started to make plans to move *Pirates* to Broadway in the fall. This seemed like a terrific idea to me, even though it meant leaving behind my barely-moved-into new house, friends, and romantic attachments. Peter Asher, always a more practical thinker than I was, reminded me that it would also interrupt the lucrative album-tour, album-tour routine that we had settled into so comfortably over the last few years.

Another problem was this: Peter and Joe Papp did not hit it off from just about the first minute they set eyes on each other. This situation eventually improved, as both were men of their word and thorough professionals, but in the beginning, it was awkward. Peter's refined manner brought out Joe's inner street fighter. I begged Peter to let me do the first round of negotiating with Papp by myself, and then he could close the deal. This, of course, was a preposterous idea, as artists can't really advocate for themselves very effectively. I told Peter that I just wanted to move with the show to Broadway and wasn't trying to get rich doing so. He muttered in response that he didn't want me to get poor, then threw up his hands and let me have my way.

A few days later, Joe came to my apartment to discuss the move to Broadway. He brought along a cigar and a couple of Spike Jones records. Rex and I had been hanging out there for a couple of hours, listening at top volume to Mick Jagger singing "Beast of Burden" on the Rolling Stones' *Some Girls* album. Joe immediately imposed order by putting on Spike Jones, the American screwball comedy bandleader of the forties and fifties, and we spent the next hour on the floor howling with laughter. Rex was also a Spike Jones fan. Then Joe lambasted us with puns for another half hour. He was fiendishly good at this. After that, it was time to get down to business, so Rex went home, and Joe got out the cigar.

I told Joe that I was in negotiations to buy an apartment so that I would have a place of my own when we moved to Broadway. The apartment belonged to the actress Liv Ullmann. In addition to acting in my favorite Ingmar Bergman movies, Ullmann had recently sung and danced for Joe Papp in a production of *I Remember Mama,* and had lived in the apartment while doing so. I figured she must have been making enough to cover her expenses there. Also, though Liv Ullmann wasn't necessarily a name on Broadway, she was highly successful in another area of the business, so I felt that our two situations were comparable. I won't even bother to point out the ways in which this was ridiculous logic. Inside, Joe must have been cackling at my naiveté. I asked for the same salary that Ullmann got. Of course, I had no way of knowing what she got, and don't to this day. To Peter's and my own utter amazement, Joe wound up making a generous offer that included some perks I never would have thought to ask for in the first place. Maybe he was surprised by my lack of aggression and didn't want to be thought of as less than a gentleman while conducting business on such an uneven playing field. Anyway, we made a deal.

The move to Broadway was reasonably smooth. There was a cast change, as Patricia Routledge was not available for the Broadway run. Veteran actress Estelle Parsons replaced her and received excellent notices for her portrayal of the daffy nursery maid, Ruth. Previews of the show started in the fall, and we opened officially at the Uris Theatre on West Fifty-First Street on the eighth of January, 1981.

For a period of time during previews, we were rehearsing one version of the show in the afternoon and performing another at night. This was exhausting, as we performed eight shows a week, and with rehearsals added, it was like doing sixteen. In addition to the rehearsals, they added performances on the *Today* show and *Saturday Night Live*. This meant getting up at four in the morning for the *Today* show and staying up till four in the morning to perform on *SNL*. We played a matinee performance on Christmas Day, and by New Year's Eve, we were completely fried. We had already done a matinee that afternoon, and in between shows, the pit band went out and got very drunk. (Who could blame them?) Rex and I, painfully sober, were staggering from fatigue around the stage with shredded vocal cords. Exotic, unfamiliar sounds emanated from the orchestra pit. The trumpet player, playing the lead into Rex's and my tender duet at the end of act one, was either a lot more hammered than the others or more nakedly exposed. He sounded truly awful. And loud.

Giggling is a plague on the nervous system that I believe is hardwired into some people's physiology and seems to be a reaction to tremendous nerves, fatigue, or self-consciousness. It is rarely a welcome occurrence to the giggler and can feel like going over Niagara Falls without a barrel. Rex and I started to giggle at the horrifying trumpet notes and couldn't get ourselves under control. The worst sin that an actor can commit is to break character onstage. This shatters the spell for the audience, and it becomes nearly impossible to win them back. Our audience, having forked over their hard-earned cash for tickets to see our now hopelessly unprofessional performance, was not amused. They began to boo. Rex and I, still struggling with our nervous system's tantrum and meltdown, finished up our songs the best we could and fled the stage.

Backstage, Rex's eyes were wide with terror and genuine anguish. I was wringing my hands in mortification. Wilford Leach was extremely concerned, and to his credit did not scream at us, though he would have been justified in doing so. He told me to change into my second act costume and, with Rex holding my hand, go out onto the stage before the show recommenced and apologize to the audience. It was absolutely the right thing to do, but it felt like going before a firing squad. I have no idea what I said to the audience, but it paved the way for the second act to begin, and we finished the show without further incident.

Until I went to work in *Pirates*, I had never had any formal voice training. The show's vocal demands were considerable, and a wonderful voice teacher, Marge Rivingston, known as "Magic Marge," was brought in to work with the entire cast.

She played mother hen, psychiatrist, and taskmaster to us all, and seemed to always have the right piece of advice, whether personal or professional, to get each of us through the show.

Bill Elliott had the girls' chorus belting high notes that originally had been written to be sung in the upper extension of the voice—where an operatic soprano sings. It sounded funnier that way, and more like the contemporary pop style that Wilford Leach had envisioned for the show. Eight performances a week of belting high notes could have created serious vocal problems for the chorus were it not for Marge's careful guidance.

My problem was the opposite. From all those years of screaming over a rock band, I had an overdeveloped belt range and an underdeveloped upper extension. Because my boy soprano brother Peter was my earliest influence, my high voice sounded more like a choirboy's than that of a grown-up lady opera singer. Rex and I, coming from rock backgrounds, had developed the unfortunate habit of muscling our way through difficult vocal territory and, for lack of a better word, yelling. Marge went to work to unravel these problems. The biggest obstacle facing us was that the Broadway schedule allows only one day a week to rest, and that is not enough time for vocal recovery. I was trying to learn a healthier singing technique while I was performing the show, and the new muscles were trying to gain strength but with not enough time to rest. My voice eventually collapsed, and I missed five shows. This is something a Broadway performer tries his or her hardest to avoid. There are a number of reasons to do so: the show loses money from ticket cancellations if the star does not appear, the dynamic between the performers is greatly altered when a new person comes in, and the feeling is that the missing cast member has let down the entire production. I got back on the stage the minute I could squeak. My voice, with Marge's coaching, eventually gained enough strength to carry me through the grueling schedule. I never missed another performance.

15

Jerry Wexler and the Great American Songbook

In the recording studio with Jerry Wexler,
listening to a playback of our ill-fated
attempt at recording standards.

I LOVED WORKING IN *Pirates,* and loved the fact that I didn't have to travel every night to a new city, but by early spring 1981, I was eager to explore some new music. I felt that I needed to do some work on my phrasing—the area of my musicianship that I had always felt was my weakest—so that I could be a stronger singer when I eventually returned to pop music. My usual method for trying to improve musically was to study what came before whatever I was interested in improving. The pop singers that came before me were the interpreters of the American standard song. I started thinking about the records that my father had brought home to play on the big high-fidelity monaural record player he bought in 1957: Ella Fitzgerald and Louis Armstrong duets, Peggy Lee, Chris Connor, June Christy, and Billie Holiday.

While in New York, I had become friendly with Jerry Wexler and his wife, Renee, whom I had known slightly when she worked for David Geffen and Elliot Roberts. Wexler was one of the most respected A&R men in the record industry. He had started out in the 1940s as a writer for *Billboard* magazine, where he coined the term "rhythm and blues" to replace the unsavory "race records." Then, in 1953, he became partners with Ahmet Ertegun and his brother, Nesuhi, and together they built the Atlantic recording label, signing culture-bending giants such as Ray Charles, Aretha Franklin, Chris Connor, Dusty Springfield, Wilson Pickett, and Led Zeppelin. Needless to say, he had a fabulous record collection. One evening I mentioned to him that I wanted to spend some time studying the singers who had reigned before rock and roll changed everything, and he offered the privileges of his vinyl treasury.

In addition to a titanic career, Wexler had a quirky charm, which he leavened with hipster street phrases and penetrating insights. At sixty-four, he spoke like a Jewish bebopper with a Jesuit education. His ears stuck out a little, like an animal on alert, giving one the impression that he was listening carefully. I was keeping steady company with journalist Pete Hamill, and Wexler expressed his wholehearted approval by describing Hamill as his favorite kind of fellow: "an educated cat from a bad neighborhood." I loved hearing Wexler's stories about the musicians, composers, thugs, and hangers-on that he had encountered in his long turn at the hub of the business. He was an ideal mentor.

Hamill, too, possessed an impressive collection of records, mostly jazz. He turned me on to players like tenor saxophonist Lester Young and trumpet player Clifford Brown, both of whom I loved for their lyrical playing styles. He had beautiful taste, and when he was writing, he always had something irresistible on his turntable. In addition to jazz, he'd sometimes play songs by the great Mexican composer Cuco Sanchez. I used some of them years later on my Mexican records. He brought me a female rendition of "What's New," which was a little closer to my key than the Sinatra version, and a stunning recording of Betty Carter singing "Tell Him I Said Hello," which I recorded in 2004, with John Boylan and George Massenburg producing. Hamill's input was indispensable.

One day Wexler and I were wandering together through the recordings of Mildred Bailey, a jazz vocalist from the 1930s, and it occurred to me that I should start making a serious effort to learn the songs. I thought I should put together a rehearsal band so that I could really work on the phrasing. Wexler offered to help me do it. Next thing I knew, we were making a record.

We started on an exploratory basis, working in the afternoons before I had to go to the theater to sing *Pirates*. Wexler assembled an excellent band of seasoned jazz players, many of whom had worked with the original interpreters of the genre. They included guitarist Tal Farlow, trumpeter Ira Sullivan, and the great pianist Tommy Flanagan. I thought we would go into the studio and rehearse and craft the arrangements as we went along. Wexler had other ideas and hired saxophonist Al Cohn to draw up the charts. Unfortunately, Al, who was a really good arranger, hadn't had any input from me before he wrote the charts, and I stumbled over some of the songs that were arranged at a brisk tempo, when I had imagined them slow and brooding. Sections of songs I would have preferred to sing rubato were tethered firmly to the rhythm section. "Never Will I Marry," a song I had wanted to sing for years, moved at such a breakneck pace that there was no room for me to swallow or breathe, let alone phrase. Wexler thought it sounded fine. I began to worry that we were not a good match in the studio, and that maybe I had jumped in too soon. He had an unfortunate habit of leaning on the talk-back mike, interrupting me in the middle of a song to give suggestions about my interpretation. I considered the interpretation to be my exclusive domain, so I wasn't happy about that, either.

I finished out my run in *Pirates* and returned to the West Coast. Wexler flew out with our master tapes, and we played the rough mixes for Joe Smith, another legendary record man, then president of my label. Smith and Peter Asher thought the project was a mistake from the beginning and didn't think the tracks should be released. I agreed with them about the tracks, but I loved the songs and still wanted to record them. Wexler thought the recording was great and argued vigorously in favor of releasing it. He wanted to finish mixing it, and out of respect for his towering position in the business, we agreed to let him, even though I knew it wouldn't affect our final decision.

What made me certain that our differences were irreconcilable was learning that he meant to leave the mixing process entirely up to the engineer, with neither of us in attendance. The mixing process can fundamentally change the sound and the emotional impact of a recording and is much too important to be left up to someone else. It can't save a bad recording, but it can destroy a good one. Working with Peter, not only did I have a lot of input into creating the arrangements, but also he and I mixed the records together with our engineer. Wexler was very cavalier about this, and told me that he often listened to the mixes over the phone and gave his final comments. He suggested that I could listen to them over the phone also and make any suggestions I wanted. I was stunned. The telephone can't begin to carry the full range of sound. One might as well use string and a paper cup. I realized that either he didn't know the difference, or he thought that *I* didn't know the difference. Either scenario was unacceptable.

After talking to some musician friends who had worked on Wexler's past productions, I realized why he had acted as he did. Wexler was, in the truest sense, an old-fashioned A&R man. In the earlier days of record making, the A&R man might select the material and musical setting for an artist such as, for instance, Rosemary Clooney. He would say to her, "I have this song, 'Come On-a My House.' We're going to record it in this style with this arranger and these musicians." Rosemary, a wonderful singer with, I assume, plenty of ideas of her own, had very little to say about it. Artists like Bob Dylan and the Beatles changed all that. They wrote or selected their own material and musical direction, becoming enormously successful in the process. David Geffen's label, Asylum, was founded on the premise that the artist's vision would be respected and supported.

Wexler was, in the best sense of the word, a great Monday morning quarterback. He could recognize when something was good after the fact. He could suggest and organize a general musical direction, but musical particulars and engineering decisions were left to specialists upon whom he relied heavily. Perhaps more heavily than he realized.

In my case, hindsight shows that his A&R instincts were correct in thinking that I could have success recording standards from the American songbook, but he couldn't execute the recording in a way that was satisfactory to me or my record label. I had to tell him the album would not be released. He was hurt and angry, and I felt terrible. I was very disappointed that the project hadn't been successful, and sorrier still to lose his friendship. He and Renee had been very kind to me while I was living in New York, and I liked them both a great deal. Under the circumstances, there was no way to save the relationship.

Peter Asher and Joe Smith, while concerned about the money lost on the record, were relieved that it was not coming out, which would have necessitated, in their opinion, throwing good money after bad. They hoped that I would forget about recording selections from the American standard songbook. I didn't.

Joe Papp and Wilford Leach had decided to make *The Pirates of Penzance* into a motion picture, and Rex Smith, Kevin Kline, Tony Azito, George Rose, and I were asked to continue our roles in the film production. We were going to film in London, so the rest of the cast, which included Angela Lansbury, would be British.

We filmed at Shepperton Studios in Surrey, about forty-five minutes outside of London, through the entire winter. Because the days were so short, our schedule landed us inside the studio just before the sun came up and excused us just after it had set. I took a room with a coal fireplace at the beautiful old Connaught Hotel and tried to keep warm, washing my clothes in the bathtub on rare days off.

Pete Hamill came and stayed for a time, bringing me a steady stream of books that he bought from a store in Charing Cross. I read them on the set waiting to be called in front of the camera: Henry James, Edith Wharton, Thomas Hardy, Flaubert, Turgenev, Zola. They provided a richer and more sophisticated context for the clownish Victorian operetta I was singing. It also gave me this wonderful line from Flaubert: "Be regular and orderly in your everyday life, like a bourgeois, so you can be violent and original in your work." I've never quite managed to match either end of this equation, but it's something to shoot for.

One day my father called and told me in a tight, gray voice that my mother, who had been ill for some time, had died. On the following day off, when I was washing my clothes in the bathtub, I remembered when I was three, following my mother down the little path to the clothesline, and handing her clothespins while she hung out the family wash. It always included the blue calico dress and tiny white pinafore worn by my Raggedy Ann doll.

As we were moving into spring, I set out one morning in the dark for my usual lengthy commute. Missing my mother and still feeling disappointment about my lost opportunity to sing the beautiful songs I had chosen for the ill-fated Wexler album, I was listening to a cassette of my old favorite Sinatra album, *Only the Lonely.* Just as Sinatra was beginning his flawless rendition of "Guess I'll Hang My Tears Out to Dry," the sun, adhering to its new spring schedule, popped its head up over the horizon. The sunlight and the music filled me, a desert dweller stranded in the cold, dark North, with longing and joy. I suddenly became aware that if I didn't record those songs that I loved, I would spend the rest of my life feeling I had missed an essential experience. I resolved to beg Peter to help me, and, against his better judgment, he agreed.

In his practical hat, Peter managed to convince me that we had better first record an album with the more contemporary music my audience had come to expect from me. I quickly began to gather material for a new record, *Get Closer.* Our regular engineer, Val Garay, wasn't available, so I suggested to Peter that we try George Massenburg, the engineer I had recorded with in Maryland. Peter had never worked with George before, but he liked the Complex, a new studio that George had recently built in West Los Angeles.

In the industry, George was regarded as one of the great pioneers of computer-automated mixing, and he was the inventor of modern equalization, which he'd developed as a teenager in his garage in Baltimore. He wore a look of quizzical befuddlement resembling the glassy-eyed stare of a stuffed animal. He didn't dress like a rock and roller, wearing instead a standard boy's haircut, crewneck sweaters, and chinos. Handsome and awkward, self-effacing and shy, George was able to run simultaneous functions in his brain, ranging from a volcanic level of creativity to a cosmic snooze. While working with him day after day in front of the enormous recording console he had designed, I sometimes felt I was sitting next to an unattended steam boiler that was overheating and dangerously close to exploding. The atmosphere in his studio reminded me of the Japanese anime classic *Howl's Moving Castle*, every track on the console a doorway into a different world of its own. What I was able to learn from him fundamentally changed the way I approached singing, recording, and listening.

I made my first digital album, *Mad Love*, in 1980. Because digital recording was a new technology then, Peter and I had not fully explored the broad range of possibilities that it offered. For instance, with analog recording, we had never developed a very sophisticated way to improve my vocal performances. As a result, most of my vocal tracks up until then had stayed exactly as I had sung them while we were recording the basic track. As we often worked on one song for hours, I would have to hold back to save my voice. Also, I was less inclined to take chances, because I was afraid I would be stuck with an idea that hadn't turned out right. The new technology greatly enhanced the ability to switch among many takes of different vocal approaches and edit together the best bits. We could drop in the most microscopic segments: a breath, a final consonant, a syllable that had wavered out of tune. A brilliant engineer like George, with his ability to hear sound in tremendous detail, knew how to match the pieces so that the edits were invisible and the singing sounded completely natural. This freed me to relax and sing anything that I wanted without having to worry that I would be stuck with something I didn't like. It also gave me a way to study the way my voice interfaced with the instrumental track, and I learned to phrase better and refine and develop new vocal textures. In short, what George had presented to me was a way to learn how to sing. We continued to work together for many years, and the learning never stopped. Peter worked beautifully with George, and the three of us became a comfortable team.

16

Nelson Riddle

*In concert with Nelson Riddle
in Santa Barbara.*

I WOKE UP IN the bedroom of my house on Rockingham Drive thinking, "Today Nelson Riddle is coming to my house, and I am going to sing Irving Berlin's beautiful song 'What'll I Do?'" A big smile spread across my face. I sank deeper into the covers and ran through the song in my mind: "What'll I do? / When you are faaar . . . away . . ." The song unspooled its loveliness in spare poetry and three-quarter time.

I jumped out of bed and hurried to take a bath and dress. I had waited so long for this. I didn't want to be the cause for any more delays.

I had decided that I would like to make my standards record with an orchestra instead of a horn band. I'd complained to Pete Hamill that I wanted the orchestrations to sound like Nelson Riddle but didn't know of any arranger who could write like him. He suggested sensibly, "Why don't you just call Nelson Riddle?" The idea hadn't occurred to me. There were several reasons:

a. I didn't know if he was still alive. (Easy enough to check.)
b. I didn't know if he knew *I* was alive, or cared.
c. I imagined that he didn't like music with rock under-pinnings and would not be interested in working with a singer from that genre.

When Peter Asher called him, it turned out that Nelson, then sixty, didn't really know who I was. He asked his daughter, Rosemary, if she thought he should work with me. "Well, Dad, the check won't bounce," was her reply. She urged him to consider it. Despite the fact that he had written arrangements for some of the greatest singers in popular music, including Nat "King" Cole, Ella Fitzgerald, Peggy Lee, Rosemary Clooney, and of course, Sinatra, Nelson's phone hadn't been ringing that much in the past several years. The rock-and-roll revolution had swept away most of his employment, and he had been surviving by writing TV music and the occasional film score.

He met us at the Complex, where Peter, George, and I were working on the final mixes for *Get Closer*. I told him how much I admired his work on Sinatra's *Only the Lonely* and what it had meant to me over the years. We played him our mix of "The Moon Is a Harsh Mistress," one of the songs on *Get Closer*. I told him that my mother had died very recently, and the song made me think of her, because when I was a little girl, I had always seen her face in the moon. He replied that his mother had died while he was working on *Only the Lonely*, and there was a lot of her in those arrangements. I asked him timidly if he would consider arranging a few tracks for me on my upcoming standards record. To ask for more seemed presumptuous. Nelson replied that the Beatles had once asked him to write an orchestral arrangement for a track on one of their albums. He had firmly declined, saying that he didn't do tracks, only albums. I whipped out the list of songs I had chosen. "Could you do all these?" I asked. He said he could.

We raced over to the piano. The first song on the list was "Guess I'll Hang My Tears Out to Dry." Nelson fished around in his briefcase and produced the original sketch of the orchestration he had done for Sinatra. Of course, it wouldn't be the right key. We experimented a little and found the one that worked for me. He crossed out Sinatra's key and wrote in mine. Our work had begun. Nelson took the sketch home to start a new arrangement in the new key. I was floored by the experience.

I told Nelson that I liked a very custom fit for my arrangements and liked to be involved from the beginning. He welcomed the idea. The morning he came to my house, lugging the heavy briefcase, we worked at the piano for a few hours, mostly choosing keys and tempos. I gave him general guidelines, leaving the musical intricacies of the orchestrations up to him. To do more was far beyond my capability. Sometimes I suggested where I wanted a rubato feeling with only strings and woodwinds *here*, bring the rhythm section back in *there*. While we were working out "Guess I'll Hang My Tears Out to Dry," I asked for a modulation to a higher key, to give the arrangement a lift. Nelson surprised me by showing me a way to modulate to a *lower* key, providing an elegant shift of mood.

When we had finished rehearsing, we sat together on the sofa and chatted about our lives. I told him about an unrequited crush I had on a composer we both knew; he told me about the great love he'd had for singer Rosemary Clooney and the torch he had carried for many years. He told me about Irving Berlin proposing to the girl he loved, and the marriage being forbidden by her father, breaking his heart and inspiring him to write "What'll I Do?" Happily, they later married. We became friends.

Before we started to record *What's New*, Joe Smith came to my house to make one final attempt to talk me out of it. He was genuinely concerned that my audience wouldn't like it and that my career would never recover from the damage. He felt that I was throwing away my professional life with both hands. By all reasonable means to assess the situation, he was right. Joe Smith was a great record man. He was a person I respected, admired, and trusted. Ordinarily I would have been inclined to listen to him. Fortunately, I had the songs of the Gershwins, Rodgers and Hart, and Irving Berlin blaring in my head and couldn't hear a word he said.

He could see that his argument was having no effect on me. I said to him, "I have Nelson Riddle on board, you know. He has agreed to write my arrangements." Smith just sighed, then he asked if he could come to the recording sessions. He loved Nelson Riddle.

We began recording on June 30, 1982. I was nervous—and had good reason to be. The enormous cost of working with a forty-piece orchestra meant that I wouldn't be able to rehearse with it beforehand, and we wouldn't be able to spend hours working on one song, building it a few tracks at a time the way we had recorded "You're No Good." It would be the first time I had actually heard the arrangements that Nelson had created for me. We would make three or four passes on each tune, and move to the next one, expecting to get three or four tunes recorded in a three-hour session. I wouldn't have time to become comfortable with the arrangements or refine them to match my vocal idiosyncrasies. Also, Nelson's intricate compositions required the ability to stretch and breathe, moving freely through time, making it, in many cases, too difficult to redo the vocals later. I was going to be stuck with my live vocals again.

We started with "What's New." First we ran through the arrangement for the benefit of the orchestra. We started recording, and I sang it three times. We used the first take and kept the vocal. This meant that what wound up on the record was me singing the song for the first time ever with that arrangement, and in that key.

My guitar-playing ability being limited to three-chord songs, I was not capable of accompanying myself on such sophisticated material. In order to practice it before the session, I had to sing along with someone else's recording, with a different arrangement and not in my key. No wonder Joe Smith had been worried. Fortunately, I was sufficiently distracted by how much I loved the music to stop worrying and just sing. Singing with Nelson's sumptuous arrangements was like swimming in cream.

Eventually, with the clock spilling money and the need to race through the songs pressing on me, my courage began to fail. John David Souther came by the studio, listened to several tracks, and gave us an enthusiastic response. I suppose he could have been just trying to be nice, but I knew that he loved the material and Nelson's work as much as I did and would know if we were not handling it with the respect and care it deserved. John David's vote of confidence was also reassuring to Peter Asher, who, being British, was not as familiar with the material and had experienced it mostly in elevators. This had placed Peter in the uncomfortable position of having to work tremendously hard to help me do something that he didn't think was a good idea to start with, while working in an unfamiliar context. He didn't complain about it and did his usual meticulous job.

Now, if by chance I'm in a store or a restaurant and hear one of those vocals that I sang in such a rush, it sounds like a sketch. I wish I'd had the luxury of performing them onstage for a few weeks before recording them, so that I could have fleshed out my phrasing ideas and sung them with more confidence, but it was not to be, and I have to accept that.

The next hurdle was figuring out how to convince my concert audience to buy tickets for a show that wouldn't include any of my previous hits and featured music of an entirely different style and generation. I hired a group of seven excellent — in some cases, legendary (bass player Ray Brown, sax player Plas Johnson) — jazz musicians to replace my regular touring band, keeping only the extraordinarily versatile keyboard player, Don Grolnick. I felt honored to play with these guys and more than a little intimidated. I added a forties-style vocal group called the Step Sisters. The nine songs I had recorded with Nelson weren't enough to fill out a whole concert. Also, singing with the Step Sisters added a section of uptempo songs to make the show a bit livelier.

My sister, Suzy, had gone to high school in the fifties. Being a pretty and popular girl, she had attended the senior prom three years of the four. She wore beautiful waltz-length "formals" with fitted strapless bodices and full skirts constructed of many layers of tulle. I loved those dresses, but by the time I got to high school in the sixties, we wore sleeveless brocade Jackie Kennedy dresses to the prom. I felt I had missed out. I hired a stylist, Jenny Shore, to hunt through the secondhand stores to find old fifties tulle prom dresses. The Step Sisters and I wore them in the show.

We opened the first performance at New York's Radio City Music Hall on September 24, 1983. Wearing my fluffy-skirted vintage prom dress, I stood in the wings holding Nelson's hand. Nelson, normally sanguine, was as nervous as I was. He squeezed my hand. "Don't let me down tonight, baby," he said. Then he pulled up the sleeve of his jacket, to show me the cuff links he wore. "You see these?" he said. "Rosemary [Clooney] gave them to me, and I always wear them when I need some luck."

We began the show with me onstage with a piano only. I sang the verse to "I've Got a Crush on You," and then Nelson and the orchestra rose from the pit on a hydraulic platform and joined me for the refrain: "I've got a crush on you, sweetie-pie / All the day and nighttime, hear me sigh."

The audience loved it, but I was unable to tell.

Peter, realizing that I was in a state of nervousness that bordered on the psychedelic, came back during the intermission to tell me we were a success. Nerves are something most performers deal with every night. I remember only the extreme cases, where time is distorted and I feel like I am standing next to my body. This was one of those times. As the old saying goes, I was beside myself.

I got through the second half of the show and went home to the little apartment I had lived in during *Pirates*. I climbed into the window seat in my tiny living room, where I could see over the Museum of Natural History to Central Park beyond. I knew that having success with the orchestra show meant that I would no longer be confined to the monotony of singing the same old songs. I had new old songs now, and the mother lode of the Great American Songbook to mine. I had chewed my way out of the trap. I smiled.

What's New, released the same month, sold over three million copies, spending eighty-one weeks on the *Billboard* album chart. Rock-and-roll diehards in the music press wondered why I had abandoned Buddy Holly for the Gershwins. The answer is that there was so much more room for me to stretch and sing. Working in *Pirates* had developed my head voice; singing standards gave me a way to marry it to my chest voice to form what voice teachers call singing in a "mix." This gave me a tremendous vocal flexibility that I hadn't had before, and I felt I was finally learning to sing. The sophisticated sweep of melody and complex layers of meaning in the lyrics meant that I could tell a richer and more nuanced story—and the story wasn't stranded in the passions of adolescence. Besides, I couldn't bear the idea that such beautifully crafted songs would be condemned to riding up and down in elevators.

There was another reason I embraced standards with such fervor. I never felt that rock and roll defined me. There was an unyielding attitude that came with the music that involved being confrontational, dismissive, and aggressive—or, as my mother would say, ungracious. These attitudes came at a time when the culture was in a profoundly dynamic state. Kids were coming of age, searching for an identity, and casting off many of the values and customs embraced by previous generations. This wasn't all bad; many of these things needed changing. (I was particularly glad to see panty girdles hit the trash heap.) Like the girls in the Weimar Republic of the 1920s who were liberated by their lack of dowries, I am happier to live in a world where birth control is readily available and a woman's right to terminate a pregnancy vigorously protected. Still, I cringe when I think of some of the times I was less than gracious. It wasn't how I was brought up, and I didn't wear the attitude well. Being considered, for a period in the seventies, as the Queen of Rock made me uneasy, as my musical devotions often lay elsewhere.

My candidate for consideration as the first fully realized female rocker is Chrissie Hynde of the Pretenders. She has the musicianship, originality, seductively cool attitude, and guitar chops to secure her place in the tradition. My crown, however tenuously it hovered above my head, is off to her. Singing standards gave me the flexibility to explore my mother's gentler nature, just as singing traditional Mexican music allowed me to explore my father's passionate, romantic side.

Nelson and I made two more records together, *Lush Life* and *For Sentimental Reasons*, but as we were finishing the third one, we discovered that he was going outside to lie down in his car during the breaks. He had become seriously ill with a liver disease and died after completing the arrangements, in October 1985. We did the final recording session without him. Some of the musicians were in tears, including his son, Christopher, who played trombone in the horn section.

Listening to the last arrangements Nelson wrote before he died, I have no doubt that he was staring at his approaching demise and trying to fortify himself with the best weapon he had, which was his music. Nelson often said that an arranger had only a few bars in which to tell his own story: usually during the intro and sometimes a section at the end. The rest of the time, he was supporting the singer's story or fleshing out the songwriter's ideas. The beginning and ending of the arrangement for the song "'Round Midnight" hold clues to what was on Nelson's mind in those final days.

Shortly after he died, I received a letter from Rosemary Clooney inviting me to sing at a benefit concert she put on in Los Angeles every year. I sent her a note that I had written with my fountain pen saying I would love to do it, and that Nelson had spoken of her often and fondly. She replied with a handwritten note inviting me to dinner at her house, saying she would love to hear about Nelson.

I was dressed and ready to leave for Rosemary's when Jerry Brown came by unexpectedly. I told him I was on my way out to dinner, and he said he was hungry and wanted to go too. I called Rosemary and asked if it would be all right to bring Jerry, and she said it was fine. As we were getting ready to leave, Jerry noticed a large box of roses someone had sent to me sitting on the table in my entryway. Probably feeling a little sheepish about inviting himself to dinner, and being a person who is notoriously tight with a dollar, he picked them up and said, "We can take these to Rosemary."

"But they're mine!" I protested.

He shot me a mischievous grin. "If I take the card out, they'll be hers."

The flowers went with us to Rosemary's house. She and her longtime companion, Dante DiPaolo (they eventually married), had made a spaghetti dinner. Her youngest daughter, Monsita, plus daughter-in-law Debby Boone, the singer, and daughter of Pat Boone, were also in attendance. We had a hilarious time. Monsita, Jerry, and I traded stories about being terrorized by the nuns in Catholic school. Between fits of laughter, Rosemary pointed her finger at me and said, "Let me tell you something: you're going to be in my life for the rest of it!" And I was. Rosemary and I became warm friends. We sang together, and she told me stories about her life and career. She also commiserated with me about the particular problems that come with living a life on the road. I used to tell her that if there were a Girl Singers Anonymous, she would be my sponsor.

Rosemary was often referred to as "the best friend a song ever had," because she had a rare ability to sing a song you'd heard a million times and make you think it was the first time you'd ever noticed its full meaning. Seemingly worn-out songs, in Rosemary's care, could suddenly blossom and make me cry.

One night, when I was at her house, she showed me a beautiful gold and emerald pin that Nelson had given her. She gave it to me to keep. I always thought that my friendship with Rosemary was a final gift from Nelson.

⟿

Jerry Brown and I had a lot of fun for a number of years. He was smart and funny, not interested in drinking or drugs, and lived his life carefully, with a great deal of discipline. This was different from a lot of the men I knew in rock and roll. I found it a relief. Also, he considered professionally many issues that I considered passionately: issues like the safety of nuclear power plants, agricultural soil erosion, water politics, and farm workers' rights. Neither of us ever suffered under the delusion that we would like to share each other's lives. I would have found his life too restrictive, and he would have found mine entirely chaotic. Eventually we went our separate ways and embraced things that resonated with us as different individuals. He finished his second term as governor in 1983 and went to work with Mother Teresa in India. I moved to New York City and went to work for Joe Papp. Jerry is back in politics now as California's governor once again and happily married to a woman I like very much. We have always remained on excellent terms.

Wearing my Mexican china poblana costume.

17

Sueños

MY FATHER CALLED FROM Tucson. He said that Lola Beltrán, my favorite Mexican ranchera singer since childhood, was going to appear at the 1983 Tucson International Mariachi Conference, an annual event then in its second year. As I had never seen her perform, he wondered if I would like to go. I jumped on a plane and flew to Tucson.

Lola was magnificent. A tall, handsome woman with strong cheekbones, she commanded the stage, her beautiful hands moving so gracefully that they were a show in themselves. Her costumes were exquisitely pretty and finely made, based on regional tradition. She moved her peach-colored silk rebozo into various poses with such elegant style that it made her simple stage production seem elaborate. Her voice was as powerful as an opera singer's, but she used it in a completely different way. She sang mostly in her huge belt voice but would crack into a soaring falsetto, purposely emphasizing the break in the voice that a classical singer will try to conceal. This is a tradition in Mexican singing, and a difficult one, usually best executed by male singers. Lola handled it effortlessly. She had a tremendous dynamic range, from a whispered, caressing murmur, to an anguished wail that could blow down the walls. Her voice was passionately sorrowful and hurdled over the language barrier to rip your heart out.

I was introduced to her afterward. When told that I was a

singer also, she presented me with the peach-colored rebozo. Later I wore it to the studio when I recorded in Spanish. It gave me courage.

Her show left me wondering where in Los Angeles I might connect with good musicians who could play the ranchera style, plus have the patience to let me hang out with them and learn. I had sung Mexican songs along with the family as a child but usually knew only a few phrases of lyrics and then would hum and "La-la-la" through the parts I didn't know. To acquire professional competence in this style would be a vertical climb.

While still thinking about the Mexican music, I got a call from Joe Papp. He was going to present Puccini's opera *La Bohème* at the New York Public Theater in the fall of 1984. He wanted me to sing the role of Mimi. Wilford Leach was going to direct. I said yes. I didn't stop to consider the difficulty. I had loved *Bohème* since childhood, hearing it frequently played and discussed at my grandparents' house. My grandmother had a recording with the Spanish soprano Victoria de los Angeles singing the part of Mimi, still my favorite interpretation. My grandfather would sit at the piano and play through the melodies, with one of my aunts chiming in on part of an aria. It seemed like family music. I was keen to start learning it.

Shortly after that, I was in New York with Randy Newman to film a television special of Randy and his music that included me and Ry Cooder. We were walking in the summer heat along Columbus Avenue on Manhattan's Upper West Side, on our way to have lunch at the Café des Artistes. I loved to eat there so that I could look at the Howard Chandler Christy murals of frolicking nude maidens on the walls.

While we were walking, a police officer ran past us at full speed, breathing hard and trying to catch up with someone we couldn't see. He pulled several yards ahead of us, and his gun slipped out of its holster, falling to the sidewalk. We called out to him, but he was already out of hearing range. I reached down to pick up the gun.

"No!" shouted Randy. "Leave it there!"

"What if a child picks it up?" I asked him. "Someone could get hurt."

"Throw it in there!" he said, indicating a large trash can.

"It might go off and kill the poor garbage collector," I argued. I decided I would be in charge of the gun and find a way to return it to the police officer who had dropped it. After all, I was a cowgirl from Arizona. My older brother, a police officer, and my father were both master marksmen. I had learned to shoot as a child. Never mind that I am frightened to death of guns and believe in strict gun control. Randy wasn't a cowboy. He grew up in L.A.

I picked up the gun and immediately spotted two police officers driving along in a squad car. I raised my arm to hail them like a taxi and started to wave the gun in their direction. Randy, who lacked experience with firearms but had a lot of awareness of what happens to people who point guns at NYPD officers, managed to hide the gun from sight while he explained to me as tactfully as he could that I was a reckless moron. He also saved us from being a headline in the next edition of *The New York Times*.

After some rapid negotiating, we agreed to stash the gun in my purse, which was actually a metal lunch box with a picture of Roy Rogers and his faithful horse Trigger on the lid. It was not a vintage lunch box but a reproduction that was a little wider than the one I'd carried in the third grade. The gun fit perfectly. We walked over to the squad car and explained what happened. I lifted the lid slowly and offered the gun in the lunch box as though it were a gift of the Magi. Miraculously, my head was not blown off. I looked down the street and saw the other police officer, minus his gun. He was looking anxiously along the sidewalk. This added credibility to our story.

We continued on our way to the Café des Artistes. Over lunch, I mentioned to Randy that I had agreed to sing the role of Mimi in *La Bohème*. He looked concerned.

"Oh no, little Mighty Mouse," he said. Randy called me little Mighty Mouse because I sang so loud. "That might be too hard for you."

I moved back into my New York apartment and began rehearsals for *Bohème*. I realized that I should have insisted on auditioning for this production too, as it was beginning to dawn on me how difficult the singing was going to be.

I fretted out loud to director Wilford Leach, who had done such a masterful job with *Pirates*. He was used to his artists obsessing about their inadequacies, and told me to stop worrying. He still didn't like opera singing and hoped we could achieve a more "natural" sound. We almost pulled it off. Again, the rest of the cast was very good. Wilford had them relying heavily on their acting ability to communicate the story, and they were up to the task. Gary Morris, a country singer with an unusually rich voice, sang Rodolfo to my Mimi. His interpretation of the character was honest and touching, his singing natural and unaffected, musically sure-footed, and respectful of the origins of the piece. David Spencer had translated the libretto into English. He approached it like he was writing lyrics for Broadway tunes, and I thought he did a wonderful job.

The result, which opened in time for the holidays, was like a Victorian Christmas card set in motion. The story, which is devastating, and the music, which is nearly indestructible, were still very moving, in spite of the change to English and the reduced orchestration. Instead of a full orchestra, we had a tiny band of musicians playing flutes, a guitar, some strings, and a mandolin. The idea was that it should have a gritty, street theater sound. Gritty it was. The principal problem, for which I had no solution, was that my voice lacked the training for such a demanding part sung exclusively in the upper extension. Naively, I thought that if I could hear a good opera singer, I could copy the sound. I could copy Victoria de los Angeles's big sound for a couple of notes, but had not developed the musculature to sustain it through a musical line. It was like having a few words in a foreign language that one can pronounce convincingly, but no vocabulary.

The reviews, some positive, some scathing, did not include a hurrah from the all-important *New York Times*. Frank Rich, a writer I respect very much, wrote, "It's not consumption that's killing Linda Ronstadt's Mimi in the New York Shakespeare Festival's crazy-quilt production of 'La Bohème'—it's abject fear." He was dead-on.

Joe Papp was at his splendid best when he came in to bolster the stricken cast. Whatever he said gave us the determination to continue to work on our performances and try to perfect them the same way we would have done if the show were a colossal hit and bound for Broadway. "The work is all!" he told us, and then read us a comforting quote from Puccini: "Critics are capable of doing much harm, and very little good."

Thus fortified, I was able to relax and enjoy the rest of the run. I have always believed that one learns more from failure than from success.

The frustration of not being able to fully realize a musical dream is disappointing and has happened to me more than once. The consolation prize that I received from my experience in *Bohème* was this: learning the part gave me a tour of composer Puccini's mind that is not available to the mere listener. Having the chance to be in such intimate company with music of that quality was worth whatever personal anguish it cost me. Now, when I go to the opera house to hear *Bohème* in more capable hands, the intimacy remains. When Rodolfo, Mimi, Marcello, and Musetta stroll onto the stage, I feel like I am greeting old friends I have not seen for a very long time, and have missed. When I hear them sing the beautiful arias in Italian, with their immaculately trained voices, I am delighted.

I closed up my New York apartment, put it on the market, and returned to the West Coast. The idea of a Mexican record was fully present in my dreams at night. The dream world of sleep and the dream world of music are not far apart. I often catch glimpses of one as I pass through a door to the other, like encountering a neighbor in the hallway going into the apartment next to one's own. In the recording studio, I would often lie down to nap and wake up with harmony parts fully formed in my mind, ready to be recorded. I think of music as dreaming in sound.

18

Canciones de Mi Padre

*With actor and singer Daniel Valdez, who performed
with us in the Canciones de Mi Padre tour.*

TIME SPENT WITH PETE Hamill had fortified my Mexican dreams.
He had gone to school in Mexico City and had an unusual un-
derstanding of the sophisticated complexities of the Mexican art
world, with a comprehensive grasp of Mexican literature, poetry, music, and visual art. The Mexicans have a fervent appreciation of poetry and make regular use of it. It occupies a high
and ancient seat in the Mexican culture. The Aztecs called it "a
scattering of jades," jade being what they valued most, far more
than the gold for which they were murdered in great numbers
by invading Spaniards. They felt that the more profound aspects

of certain concepts, whether emotional, philosophical, political, or artistic, could be expressed only in poetry.

Mexican song lyrics, from sophisticated city cultures to the most basic rural settlements, are rich in poetic imagery. I was beginning to learn the words to the songs I had cherished since childhood and writing the English translations above the Spanish, so that I would know exactly what each word meant and be able to give it the proper emotional emphasis.

I was still casting about for someone to start teaching me the rhythmic intricacies of the songs, particularly the formidable huapangos, when I got another call from my father saying that the Tucson International Mariachi Conference had invited me to sing a few songs in its gala. The organizers were offering the famed Mariachi Vargas de Tecalitlán to accompany me, with its director, Rubén Fuentes, to write my arrangements. I was astonished! If I were singing standards, it would be like having Nelson Riddle and a full orchestra fall in my lap.

Mariachi Vargas is a band that formed in Mexico before the turn of the twentieth century and is widely considered the best mariachi in the world. Rubén Fuentes is a preeminent figure in the Mexican music business. He is a composer of many hits, and was the musical director of RCA Records in Mexico for at least a decade, producing a large number of ranchera recording artists, including Lola Beltrán. He was partners with Silvestre Vargas, son of the original leader of the Mariachi Vargas, and has produced and arranged for the band since the 1950s.

This was a tremendous opportunity, and I decided that I would try to learn three songs and figure out a way I could rehearse them before I had to go to Tucson and perform. I chose songs I knew from recordings that my father had brought from Mexico when I was about ten. I had heard them a lot but never attempted to sing them.

Rubén Fuentes flew to Los Angeles from his home in Mexico City to meet with me about the arrangements. My Spanish speaking ability is limited to the present tense, and my vocabulary is like a child's, so I begged my dear friend Patricia Casado, whose family owns Lucy's El Adobe Cafe in Hollywood, to come translate for me.

In addition to serving the best Mexican food in L.A., Patricia and her parents, Lucy and Frank, were like family to me. They were the same for any number of young musical hopefuls who recorded in the studios near their Hollywood restaurant, including the Eagles, Jackson and John David, Jimmy Webb, and Warren Zevon. We all relied on Lucy for great food and an encouraging word. She was known to tear up a check if she knew that a regular was having a bad stretch. The local police and firemen ate there, and received special consideration from Lucy, as did many journalists and politicians, including Jerry Brown, whom I met there when he was California's secretary of state. Movie industry people from the Paramount Studios across the street came too, for both the food and the camaraderie.

When I returned home from a tour, I stopped there on my way from the airport. It was my home base.

A few days before Rubén arrived in L.A., I was lifting a heavy suitcase from the baggage carousel in the airport and injured my back. I could barely walk and had to stay in bed. To cancel the meeting was out of the question, as Rubén had come a long way, with the sole purpose of meeting with me. Patricia helped me tidy my hair and find a suitable dressing gown. She helped me hobble from my bed to the pink sofa in my bedroom, and we had our meeting there. I was embarrassed to be receiving him in such a state, but there was no other choice.

He arrived with Nati Cano, who was the leader of Mariachi Los Camperos, a band closely matched to Mariachi Vargas in quality and based in Los Angeles. Rubén was in his sixties, handsome, urbane, low key, and I could tell that he was used to being in charge. Nati Cano, himself a brilliant musician and composer, would become my teacher and revered mentor for many years to come.

I showed Rubén the list of the three songs I had chosen. Two were huapangos, which, in addition to the complicated rhythm structure, require a lot of falsetto. He was surprised by my choices. "These are very old and very traditional," he said. "How did you hear them?" I told him I had heard them since childhood. "They are difficult to sing. Maybe you should pick something else." I wanted to sing the ones I had. He agreed to send the arrangements to Nati Cano, who assured me that I would be able to rehearse with the Camperos a few times before going to Tucson.

Nati Cano owned a downtown L.A. restaurant, La Fonda, where the Camperos appeared nightly. We rehearsed there in the afternoon, and I stayed to hear the show in the evening. In addition to the band, which featured one superlative singer after another, a pair of folkloric dancers performed traditional dances—"La Bamba" and "Jarabe Tapatio" being the outstanding numbers. I was much impressed by a particularly graceful young dancer, Elsa Estrada. Irresistibly charming in her beautiful white lace dress from Veracruz, she flashed her huge black eyes, heels drumming the intricate steps of "La Bamba": *"Para bailar La Bamba, se necesita una poca de gracia."* (To dance La Bamba, what is needed is a little bit of grace.)

Elsa had a bounty of grace. I decided that I wanted to put together a show in which I sang entirely in Spanish, featuring Elsa's beautiful dancing. I wanted it to be based on little vignettes of different regions in Mexico, much like my Aunt Luisa had done with her presentation of folkloric songs and dances from Spain.

The performance I did of the three songs I had chosen to perform in Tucson was rocky, but unlike my experience in *Bohème*, I felt that mastering the form was within my reach, and would simply be a matter of time and rehearsal. I found a teacher to show me the dance steps to some of the songs, so that I would be able to break down the rhythms and understand the phrasing better.

I asked Rubén if he would be interested in producing a record for me with the Mariachi Vargas, and he agreed to do it. Remembering my unhappy experience with Jerry Wexler, I decided to hedge my bet and include Peter Asher as coproducer.

When my record company heard my new plans, the people there were certain I had finally lost my mind: Record archaic songs from the ranches of Mexico? And all in Spanish? Impossible! I pleaded with them, arguing that I had sold millions of records for them over the years and deserved this indulgence. Peter was impressively game. He had never even encountered a Mexican song in an elevator, didn't speak a word of Spanish, and would be coproducing with someone who spoke almost no English. I figured they were both gentlemen, and professionals, and would work it out. I was right.

Rubén Fuentes had been involved with Mariachi Vargas during *La Epoca de Oro*, the golden era of mariachi, stretching from the thirties through the fifties. I had grown up loving those records, mostly high-fidelity monaural recordings made in the RCA Victor studios in Mexico City. They had a warm, natural sound, and I was hoping to capture some of that tradition on my own recording. Rubén was pushing for a more modern sound with plenty of echo on the violins and a more urban approach to the arrangements. I met with some resistance when I asked him to replace the modern chords with simpler one-three-five triads. Over the years, Rubén had been largely responsible for diversifying the mariachi style and cultivating a sophisticated urban sheen. To go back to a traditional style understandably seemed like regression to him, but I wanted what I had heard and loved as a child.

I had acquired a very nice black-and-white cow, Luna, who was a pet. She produced an adorable calf, Sweet Pea. I brought all the pictures I had of Luna and Sweet Pea, and tacked them up on the wall in the recording studio. I joked with Rubén in my fractured Spanish that I wanted more cows and fewer car horns in my arrangements. Rubén, who was not used to an artist having an opinion—and most certainly not a female artist—was somewhat vexed. To his credit, he made an earnest effort to compromise. I didn't want to push him too hard, because I knew he understood the audience that would buy this kind of record better than I did.

Learning to sing all those songs in another language with their enigmatic rhythms was the hardest work I've ever done. I didn't get exactly the sound I wanted from the recording, but the record-buying public didn't seem to mind. *Canciones de Mi Padre*, released in November 1987, was immediately certified double platinum, sold millions of records worldwide, and is the biggest-selling non-English-language album in American recording history. It won the Grammy for best Mexican-American Performance. I was as surprised as the record company at its success. I have to say that it succeeded on the strength of the material. The songs are strong and beautiful, and are accessible to people who have no knowledge of Spanish. There are many artists who sing the material better than I do, but I was in a position to bring it to the world stage at that particular time, and people resonated to it.

I began to scramble to put together a show. I was friendly with Michael Smuin, who had been artistic director of the San Francisco Ballet for a number of years. A terrific dancer and choreographer, he created a wonderful production of *Romeo and Juliet*, and an interpretation of *Les Enfants du Paradis*, with an Edith Piaf score, that I had adored. He choreographed several short dance pieces to tracks from my Nelson Riddle recordings for prima ballerina Cynthia Gregory, and I had the thrilling experience of performing them live with her. I had to keep my eyes closed tight when I was on the stage with Cynthia, because if I watched her, I would become mesmerized by her dancing, stand there with my mouth hanging open, and forget to sing. Michael was married to Paula Tracy, also a ballet dancer, and the ballet mistress for many of her husband's ballets. She and I were close friends.

I wanted a stage director who knew how to move groups of dancers around the stage but would respect the integrity of the traditional dances and leave them intact. I also wanted a theatrical show with good production values to frame the music and make it more understandable to an English-speaking audience.

I called another dear friend, Tony Walton, and asked if he would design my sets. Tony's movie credits included designing sets and costumes for *Murder on the Orient Express, Mary Poppins,* and *All That Jazz,* for which he won an Oscar. He was also the designer for a long list of successful Broadway shows and many of Michael Smuin's ballets. He and his wife, Gen, were close friends of the Smuins.

I began to assemble images of what I wanted the show to look like, and Michael, Paula, and I spent hours talking and dreaming together. Paula, while on a trip to Oaxaca, a state in the south of Mexico that is famous for its art, had bought a small wooden box hand-painted in black enamel, with a design bordered in pink roses and other multicolored flowers. I thought that the border design could be used for our proscenium. Tony used that idea and added many wonderful ideas of his own, including a huge fan that unfurled at the beginning of the show and a moving train for a section of songs that I sang about the Mexican Revolution. Jules Fisher came on board as lighting designer. Michael added a fogged stage lit with black light for a dance he created for a song about a ghostly ship with tattered sails ("La Barca de Guaymas"), and also came up with the idea of releasing live white doves at the end of the show. Two of the doves were trained to fly to my upraised hands and perch on my fingers. I was instructed by the dove wrangler to praise them extravagantly and tell them they did a wonderful job. They never missed a cue.

I asked Manuel Cuevas, who had designed the cowgirl outfits that Dolly, Emmy, and I had worn for the *Trio* album cover, to design my costumes. Manuel had also designed the suits worn by the Flying Burrito Brothers for Nudie, the iconic Western tailor. Most people don't realize that the fancy cowboy suits worn famously by movie stars such as Roy Rogers and Dale Evans, Gene Autry, and my childhood hero, Hopalong Cassidy, are of a traditional Mexican design. The yoked cowboy shirts with pearl snaps are worn by working cowboys in the northern Mexican states of Sonora and Chihuahua. American cowboys, particularly in Texas, Arizona, and New Mexico, adopted the styles. The cowboy hat and cowboy boots are also imported from northern Mexico and are worn regularly today by both working cowboys and gentlemen ranchers in the Sonora desert, where my grandfather was born. In Mexico, you can tell where a person comes from by the regional style of his or her clothing. Manuel, a Mexican national born in Michoacán, knew that my family's origins were in Sonora, and he dressed me accordingly. That meant ultracomfy, beautifully stitched cowboy boots with fine woolen cavalry twill skirts and embroidered cowgirl jackets. Manuel showed me how he would twist the thread while he was embroidering the design so that the embroidery would catch the lights onstage. When it comes to stage clothes, Manuel is the grand master. His designs for Elvis Presley, Johnny Cash, George Jones, Glen Campbell, and many others became the definition of the rhinestone cowboy.

The *charro* suit, worn by the mariachi, is also an equestrian costume but comes from the state of Jalisco, where the mariachi itself originates. It is the tuxedo of the wealthy landowner, who would ride the long distances between ranches to social events on horseback, his suit richly embroidered and his saddle, bridle, belt buckle, and spurs gleaming with sterling silver fittings. When my sister and I were girls, we had giddy notions of being swept away on horseback by such a man, like the heroine being abducted by her hero in the Mexican movies. When we went to balls and picnics in Mexico, my father stood close by to ensure that nothing of the sort would happen. In those days, Mexican mores were still fettered in the nineteenth century, and girls were closely chaperoned until they were married.

After I began touring regularly with the Mexican show, I would sometimes perform at a *charreada*, which is like a rodeo where charros get together to show their skills at handling stock. The charreadas include music, and the singers often perform from the back of a horse. The women riders who compete wear huge sombreros and long dresses with a double-circle fullness in their lacy skirts, and are mounted on sidesaddles. It is not considered ladylike for them to ride astride. They are extreme daredevils, executing complex maneuvers at breakneck speed, both legs draped modestly to one side, sometimes flashing a glimpse of a dainty laced boot.

When I was invited to perform at my first charreada, I knew that I would be expected to sing riding on a sidesaddle. I had never ridden on one, but my sister had, so I decided I'd be able to figure it out when I got there. The first thing I did was check out the horse they had provided for me, a big, handsome quarter horse gelding called Chulo, to make sure he wouldn't get spooked by the music. I asked one of the musicians from the mariachi to blow a loud trumpet next to his ear. Chulo didn't blink. I climbed up on his back and settled myself into the unfamiliar sidesaddle. I have ridden horses all my life, but a good comparison to that experience would be to ask a person who has driven a car all his life to drive the freeways while sitting on the steering wheel. I de-

cided the word *sidesaddle* was an anagram for *suicidal*. I was about
to jump off Chulo's back and sing my songs standing in the mud
in the center of the arena when I caught my reflection in a car
window. The combination of my big hat and skirt, sidesaddle, and
handsome horse created a dashing effect. Vanity carried the day.

I rode into the arena and began to sing. At a charreada, if the
people in the crowd like you, they will throw articles of clothing
at you. After I sang a few lines, hats, bandannas, and hoodies
began to rain on me. I was worried it might frighten Chulo, but he
took it in stride. As we rounded the first corner of the arena, the
sound system began to feed back. It was loud enough to bother
my ears, and there were surely frequencies out of the range of
human hearing that were unbearable to Chulo's sensitive equine
ears. He started to jump around, shaking his head, desperate to
get away from the high-pitched squealing. I tried to reassure him
by talking to him and patting his neck, but I also had to keep
singing. I was wearing a body mike that amplified my singing
in Spanish, but between lines of the song, it also amplified me
pleading with Chulo in English to please not kill me by bucking
me off and leaving me in the middle of the arena with a broken
neck. I finally solved the problem by steering him to the corner
opposite where the feedback was coming from and staying put.

After the show was over, I hugged Chulo and thanked him
for not throwing me off. I asked his owner if he would sell him
to me, so I could ride him in some more charreadas. The owner
responded by making the horse a gift, and Chulo came to Northern California to live with my other horses and Luna and Sweet
Pea. Unfortunately, he injured his leg in the trailer during the ride
north, and we never got to perform together in any more shows.
He spent the rest of his days in retirement, roaming acres of green
pasture with other friendly horses. I think it was a happy change
for him, as the life of a working charro horse is a tough one indeed.

We played the first show of the Canciones de Mi Padre tour in San Antonio, Texas. We had carefully advertised the show as being all in Spanish, but I didn't know if people would still be expecting to hear "Blue Bayou" and other English-language hits. The tour was booked into many of the same venues that I had played with my rock band and also with Nelson Riddle. I wasn't sure whether people would actually show up. Advance ticket sales had not been strong, and we worried it was a bad sign. As I squinted through the bright lights at the audience, I was surprised at what I saw, that night and during the entire tour: the theaters were packed, and mostly with enthusiastic brown faces. I learned that Mexican audiences generally don't buy tickets in advance but come out the night of the performance and purchase their tickets at the box office. They also bring the whole family, with grandmothers and small children in attendance. The Canciones show had attracted a completely different audience from my previous tours. They knew the songs and sang along, especially the grandparents, who had courted to many of the songs. To my relief, no one yelled for "Blue Bayou" or "Heat Wave."

The Mexican shows were my favorites of my entire career. I would sing two or three songs at a time, change costumes, and be back in time to watch the dancers. I never tired of them. The musicians were stellar and included a number of powerful singers. I learned from them every night. The members of our touring company became close immediately, and I didn't feel the loneliness that I had experienced during previous tours. Riding on the bus late at night, I would doze off to the sound of rich voices speaking in a mix of Spanish and English, just like in my childhood. After the surreal experience of being caught in the body-snatching machinery of the American celebrity juggernaut, I felt I was able to reclaim an essential part of who I was: a girl from the Sonoran Desert.

I made a second album, 1991's *Mas Canciones*, again with Rubén and Peter coproducing. Michael Smuin's wife, Paula, designed and directed a simpler version of the show, which still included the dancers and yet was flexible enough to perform in Carnegie Hall or at a state fair. I liked the simpler version even more than the elaborate one. With the dancers' colorful costume changes alone, we had plenty of production value. Mariachi Los Camperos, which became my touring band for Mexican shows for the next twenty years, performed its own section of the show and electrified the audience every night. Of the first-tier mariachis of the time, they were the most traditional, featuring silken vocal trios and sensational solo performances by Ismael Hernández, my favorite singer in the band. His powerful ranchera-style tenor hit the audience like a cannonball and would have me stomping and hollering from the wings. My favorite memory of my career as a touring performer is of sitting quietly next to Paula at the side of the stage, settling my nerves, and waiting for her to cue the lights and start the show.

19

Cry Like a Rainstorm

Photo by Robert Blakeman/Sarah A. Friedman.

AFTER SINGING EIGHT SHOWS a week in *Pirates*, struggling with *Bohème*, touring with Nelson Riddle and the orchestra, and spending another year with the Mexican show, I had found strengths and sounds in my voice that I never knew existed. I was preparing for another English-language record, and called some of my songwriter friends who had consistently delivered thoughtful, well-crafted songs. These included Eric Kaz, Karla Bonoff, and Jimmy Webb.

From singing so many drastically different styles of music, I had learned that there are infinite ways to approach the vocal production of sound and that most of the decisions about how to select them are made on an unconscious level. These decisions are constructed at great speed in some back room of the brain. They are informed by the story with the most urgent need to be told and by how that story should be framed. If it happened on a conscious level, it would be a week before a breath could be drawn to sing the first note. I would simply watch it unfold, often surprised at the result.

When singing classical pieces by composers such as Puccini, the vowels become all-important, and the sound hitches a ride on a big, open *aah* or *o*. With a standard song—for instance Rodgers and Hart's "Bewitched, Bothered and Bewildered"—one can fly through the vowels at full speed and slam into the consonants without even hitting the brakes. Beginning and ending consonants really matter. The second half of the verse to "Bewitched" is particularly rich in this regard:

> Love's the same old sad sensation [lots of sibilance and
>   alliteration to play with]
> Lately, I've not slept a wink [more sibilance and a nice
>   hard *k* to slam into]

Jimmy Webb is one of the few modern songwriters comparable to the old masters like Rodgers and Hart in songwriting craft, including the ability to write a pop song with enough musical sophistication for an orchestra to get some traction. Toward the end of his masterful "Still Within the Sound of My Voice," he provides a chance to pummel an internal rhyme scheme without mercy:

> And are you still within the sound of my *voice*
> Why don't you let me *know*, I just can't let you *go*
> If it's wrong, then I have no *choice*
> But to love you un*til* I no longer have the *will*
> Are you *still* within the sound of my *voice*

As a songwriter, Jimmy Webb kills me. His songs are difficult, but the emotional dividend is worth the risk a singer must take in scaling the tremendous melodic range his compositions explore. The payload of feelings is squeezed into the way his chords are voiced and can provoke a sharp emotional response in the first few measures of the intro, before the singer even begins. Compared to another contemporary master—say, Brian Wilson of the Beach Boys—he doesn't provide words that give easy access to a beautiful vocal sound. It is precisely this quality that lends his songs their cranky charm, whereas Brian writes lyrics that sing beautifully. When I recorded his "Don't Talk (Put Your Head on My Shoulder)" and "In My Room," I learned his songs are not easy, either, but they remind me of a beautiful horse that will give you the smoothest ride of your life if you know how to ride it. Jimmy, on the other hand, might buck you off at any turn. The sounds that result from Jimmy's lyrics are pegged to his own vocal style: a choirboy sweetness fortified by a rich har-de-har Oklahoma farm-boy twang. I love his singing.

When Peter Asher and I began to record the *Cry Like a Rain-storm* album, our best collaboration, in my opinion, Jimmy wrote an orchestral arrangement for me of his wistful song "Adios," with Brian Wilson singing the complex backing harmonies. I had known Brian briefly in my Troubadour days, when he was separated for a time from his first wife. He was always sweet and friendly, and never pressed any romantic agenda. Several times I discovered him at my back door, studying a little pile of coins he held in his hand, which he said was ten or fifteen cents shy of the price of a bottle of grape juice. He said it was important for him to drink grape juice in order to solve some health problem that was troubling him. He didn't say what it was, nor did I ask. I would provide the remaining ten or fifteen cents, and we would climb into his huge convertible with the top always down, the back stuffed with a sizable accumulation of Brian's dirty laundry. As a bachelor, he seemed to have difficulty coping with his domestic arrangements, so I would suggest a trip to the Laundromat, where we would fill an entire row of machines. (I had lots of quarters.) Afterward, we would sit in my living room, drink the grape juice, and listen to my small collection of Phil Spector records. Brian really liked Phil Spector.

In the studio, under Brian's direction, we recorded his harmony parts for "Adios" with five separate tracks of unison singing on each of the three parts, fifteen vocal tracks in all. He didn't seem concerned if some of the tracks veered slightly out of tune, but took advantage of the slight "chorused" effect it created when he came back into the control room to mix the harmony tracks into the creamy vocal smoothness instantly recognizable as the Beach Boys.

Brian was making up the harmonies as he went along, but sometimes, when he was having difficulty figuring out a complicated section, he would scold himself and say that he needed to work for a time at the piano. However, when he sat down at the piano, he never played any part of "Adios," but instead would play a boogie-woogie song, very loud, in a different key. After a few minutes of this, he would go back to the microphone and sing the parts perfectly, without a trace of hesitation.

While working with Nelson, I had gotten spoiled by the huge acoustic resonance of the orchestra and wanted more of it. Peter, whose mother had been an oboe professor at the Royal Academy of Music in London, shared my enthusiasm. For years, the trend in recording had been to record in small, dead rooms and add electronic embellishment in the form of echo and equalization. I wanted to make a record that included a lot of natural ambient room sound, and, beginning with the album *Cry Like a Rainstorm, Howl Like the Wind,* I found it in the huge scoring stage at Skywalker Sound, in Northern California, where I was living. The space, which was created for recording orchestral scores for film, really roared. Like other favorite studios where I had recorded, most notably Studio A at Capitol, it had its own distinctive sonic footprint. The room itself was an additional member of the band. I wanted a big choir for two of the songs, so I enlisted the Oakland Interfaith Gospel Choir, under the direction of Terrance Kelly. Their primary contribution was on the title track, "Cry Like a Rainstorm," George Massenburg's engineering indulging our shared passion for true high fidelity sound. It is amazing to me that, since the invention of iPods, almost no one listens to music in that format anymore. Instead of a dedicated space to hear music with big stereo speakers, sharing what one hears with others in the room, we are listening on cheesy laptop speakers or in the isolated spaces created by tiny earbuds. It makes me sad.

There was one other thing on my list: I wanted to sing with Aaron Neville.

In Los Angeles, word would spread fast whenever the Neville Brothers came to play. The musician phone tree would start humming. I would get a call from bassist Bob Glaub or guitarist Waddy Wachtel, guys who had played in my various bands. We would cancel whatever plans we had and go hear Aaron, Art, Charles, and Cyril Neville play music that has only one point of origin, and that is New Orleans. We would wait for Aaron to sing his first big hit, "Tell It Like It Is," and scream our guts out cheering. A standout for me was his searing interpretation of the haunting ballad "Arianne," which could leave me in a state of near paralysis.

The countertenor register where Aaron sings, and the five-beat West African rhythms that support him, are rooted deeply in the sophisticated eighteenth-century culture of the New Orleans Creoles. Children of wealthier families were often sent to Paris to be educated, and musical alliances were formed with French opera. The tenors of French Baroque opera sang their high notes in the falsetto register or with softly floating "head tones" instead of blasting high Cs from their chests like Italian tenors were doing by the late nineteenth century. Their styles of melismatic vocal embellishment were regional and guarded jealously. The Creoles were French-speaking and Catholic. In modern culture, their five-beat West African rhythms and falsetto high notes stand in stark contrast to the Protestant, belted styles of rhythm and blues, which places the accent on two and four (the backbeat) in a four-beat measure. (To understand five-beat, think of the famous Bo Diddley beat and clap one, two-three, one-two.) A case can be made that Aaron's singing style bears a closer relationship to French Baroque opera composer Jean-Philippe Rameau than it does to Wilson Pickett.

Too shy to navigate backstage politics and wangle an introduction to the Nevilles, I had never met them. In 1984 I went to New Orleans with Nelson Riddle to sing at the World's Fair. The night of the show, the word came from our Louisiana-born sax player, Plas Johnson, that the Nevilles were playing a late show at one of the World's Fair venues that night. When my show was finished, I hurried out of my costume and put on a cotton dress that would be comfortable in the sticky New Orleans humidity. We crammed the whole band and some of the road crew into a couple of cars and rushed over to where the Nevilles were playing. I had never seen them work to a hometown crowd, and they were steaming.

Toward the end of the set, Aaron announced that I was in the audience and said that he wanted to dedicate the next song to me. As he began to sing, I realized it was "Arianne"! I was mesmerized. After he finished the song, he invited me to come up and sing with them. This is something I never do, unless I am well acquainted with whomever is performing and have had a chance to rehearse, but after hearing Aaron sing "Arianne," I wasn't about to refuse him. I didn't have any idea what I would do once I got up there. Aaron leaned over and said they were going to sing some doo-wop. Being a soprano, I was relieved. I jumped on a falsetto high part above Aaron and held on for the ride.

The next morning, I woke up in my bed at the Royal Orleans Hotel and remembered the thrill of singing with Aaron the night before. I thought our voices sounded good together, and it might be a cool idea to record with him. Then a darker thought crowded in. *Of course* I thought it sounded good. *Anyone* sounds good when singing with Aaron Neville. I continued my tour and bent my thoughts to more attainable dreams.

A few months later, I was surprised to hear that Aaron's manager had called to invite me to sing with him at a concert to benefit an organization called New Orleans Artists Against Hunger and Homelessness. Aaron had teamed with legendary New Orleans composer and record producer Allen Toussaint, plus Sister Jane Remson, a charming, brilliant, and resourceful Catholic nun, to found the organization to bolster the state's hopelessly inadequate facilities to aid the homeless. Whatever lingering resentments I harbored about my early school experiences with the nuns at Saints Peter and Paul were swept aside by Sister Jane's blazing charm and efficient, compassionate approach to problem solving. She, along with Sister Helen Prejean, also of New Orleans, are part of a small and determined group of Catholic nuns who, in spite of the benighted and regressive attitude of the church hierarchy and its best efforts to impede them, continue to do excellent work among the less fortunate. They are my heroes.

I flew to New Orleans without much of a plan about what

I would sing when I got there. Aaron and I had both attended Catholic school and had known Franz Schubert's "Ave Maria" since childhood. My brother Peter had sung it as the featured soloist in concerts all over the country when he toured with the Tucson Arizona Boys Chorus. Aaron told me that the song had come into his mind when he was experiencing a great crisis, and he felt it had saved him. He now included it in his shows. Since we both knew the melody and all the Latin words, we decided to sing it together. Aaron remembers asking me to sign a photograph to him, and I wrote, "To Aaron, I'll sing with you anytime, anyplace, in any key." We began to discuss the idea of recording together.

I found four songs for us to sing. Two of them, "Don't Know Much," and "All My Life," became Grammy-winning hits. Aaron was nervous at the Grammy ceremony and nearly forgot his most important priority, which was to thank his beloved wife, Joel. Those affairs are often fraught with nerves and other uncomfortable feelings. It is lovely to have one's work acknowledged, but prizes have seldom mattered to me, as I generally feel that I know whether I have done well or not—and as often as not, come up short in my estimation of my performance. In that case, no prize will soothe the sting of thinking I should have done better.

The first time I won a Grammy, in 1975, I didn't expect it and had not prepared anything to say. After awkwardly mumbling a thank-you to Peter Asher and having my picture taken by members of the press, I went in search of the ladies' room. Jazz singer Sarah Vaughan was scheduled to perform at the Grammys that year, and I wanted to see her. Time was getting short, so I started running for the door of the ladies' room just as someone else was hurrying out. I smashed my face into the opening door at full speed and spent the rest of the evening sitting in the audience with a goose egg swelling on my cheekbone. For me, winning a prize means that my name is announced, I get real nervous, and then I get hit in the face.

Aaron asked me and George Massenburg to produce an album for him. He wanted very much for it to include the "Ave Maria," which had such a personal meaning for him. I suggested arranging it with a boys' choir, as that had been the way I heard my brother sing it as a child. We recorded at Grace Cathedral in San Francisco. I inserted myself as an extra boy soprano, harmonizing with Aaron toward the end of the song. People often comment that Aaron sings like an angel. In that setting, he was the mightiest of archangels.

With my daughter.

20

Living the Dream

BETWEEN THE AGES OF forty and fifty, I had a fully matured voice with a vocal toolbox that was as diverse as it was ever going to be, and I did some of my best singing. I recorded two more Grammy-winning albums, among others. They were *Frenesí* (1992), which was all in Spanish, and *Dedicated to the One I Love* (1996), a record I made for soothing my small children to sleep. I also recorded *Trio II* (1999) with Dolly Parton and Emmylou Harris, and *Western Wall: The Tucson Sessions* (1999), an album of duets with Emmylou.

One of my favorite projects during that time was the re-corded version of Randy Newman's musical *Faust*, based on the classic German legend. Eventually performed on the stage, it had a recording cast with Don Henley as Henry Faust; James Taylor as God; Elton John as Rick, an archangel; Randy as the Devil; Bonnie Raitt as Martha, a good-time girl; and me as Margaret, the ingénue who is destroyed by Faust.

Randy's songs can be bleak. Not to seem a hard man, he will insert a shard of comfort so meager it seems Dickensian. His songs are superbly crafted, with a musical tension that results from this combination of hope and utter despair. In his orches-trations, he might comment on the narrative being carried by the singer, using the instruments to deliver the jabs. Singing in the midst of one of his arrangements can feel like taking part in a boisterous discussion, with people of unevenly matched intelli-gence, sensibility, and insight ranting and squabbling. He spares himself least of all, and during recording sessions, he will make the orchestra weak from laughter, often with jokes about the inadequacies of his conducting. Whatever these inadequacies may be, he manages to get the job done, and beautifully.

After I turned fifty, my voice began to change, as older voices will. I recrafted my singing style and looked for new ways to tell a story with the voice I had. My final solo recording, 2004's *Hummin' to Myself,* was a collection of standard songs recorded with a small jazz ensemble that included cello and violin. Eugene Drucker, the violinist in the Emerson String Quartet, came to play on Alan Broadbent's arrangement of Cole Porter's "Miss Otis Regrets," which had been written for piano, violin, cello, and double bass. Drucker is a player of dazzling ability, and when he took his violin from the case and began to play, the sound boiling out of his instrument stunned us all. "What was the make of the violin he played?" we wanted to know. It was a Stradivarius, made in Cremona, Italy, in 1686. Of course, it takes a player of Drucker's ability to get the Stradivarius to sing so beautifully. Sitting next to Drucker, playing the cello, was his wife, Roberta Cooper, who plays with the Westchester Philharmonic and is another superb musician. Her cello, also from Cremona, was crafted by the famous luthier Francesco Ruggieri and is a year older than the Stradivarius. I imagined that the two instruments had met before during their long and perilous journeys through the centuries, and wondered if, in the care of this wonderfully talented couple, they felt like old friends reunited.

The final album I made before I retired from singing altogether was recorded in Louisiana with my friend Ann Savoy. The Savoys are a family of seemingly limitless talent and abilities and sit at the center of the Cajun music world. They live in Eunice, Louisiana, on a farm that has been in the Savoy family for seven generations. Ann's husband, Marc Savoy, makes the exquisitely handcrafted Acadian accordions prized by the masters of the Cajun accordion, of which Marc is one. He has been making these accordions since 1960, and when he lifts his large, handsome head to give the downbeat for a Cajun tune, he becomes one of the great gods of rhythm and joy. Marc can be prickly and moody, and Ann's friends will tease her and tell her that she married the Cajun Heathcliff. He has a degree in chemical engineering but prefers to deal with wood. He might throw his head back and roar, "Let's all get drunk and roll in the grass!" Then he will surprise you with a refined sensibility and gracious manner. I remember finding him in a rare moment when he wasn't busy cleaning a chicken, making a batch of blood sausage, or crafting yet another beautiful accordion. I told him that Ann and I had seen the recent film version of *Pride & Prejudice* with Keira Knightly, and it had inspired me to read the Jane Austen book for the umpteenth time. "Oh," he replied thoughtfully, "I just reread *Persuasion*."

Ann is a true beauty, with alabaster skin, black hair, the palest dusting of freckles, and dark eyes that slope down at the outer corners. She has a classic Greek profile with a wink of Native American in her visage. Like her husband, she is an expert on the Cajun/Creole cultures of Louisiana. She executes a slamming rhythm on her big archtop guitar, and exhibits bionic stamina playing hour after hour for Cajun dances. Virginia-born, she studied art in Paris. Ann speaks Parisian French well but can also speak and sing like a Cajun. When she is not bent over a guitar, she'll be sitting at her sewing machine, making a pretty dress to wear to the next dance or concert performance at folk festivals all over the world. The finished dress will be a design from the 1920s and look charming on her.

In addition to singing with the Savoy Family Cajun Band— composed of Ann, her husband, and their two sons—she records and performs with a group of women called the Magnolia Sisters. They sing very old Cajun songs that Ann has collected. The songs are in French and are accompanied by guitars, fiddles, and accordion. The Magnolia Sisters have a haunting, plain sound, moody harmonies, and are most wonderful when they sing in unison with no instrumental accompaniment.

Ann and Marc have two gorgeous daughters who live in Paris. Sarah plays in a Cajun band, and Anna Gabrielle is a gifted visual artist. Their sons not only play in the Savoy family band but also belong to terrific bands of their own. These bands are comprised of the younger generation of Cajun/Creole musicians devoted to the tradition. Joel, a luthier who makes guitars, also produces and records in the studio he built on the Savoy farm. He plays Cajun fiddle and Gypsy jazz guitar. His younger brother, Wilson, plays blues-inflected honky-tonk piano and bawls Ray Charles classics in French. He is an enthralling performer. There is a constant stream of homemade music coming out of Ann's kitchen, her living room, the yard where Marc is cooking something good over a fire, or the studio where the boys record.

When Ann and I met in 1989, we discovered that we had an uncanny number of things in common. We loved the same songs, as well as early-twentieth-century art, furniture, books, fabrics, and design. We even had the same teacups on our shelves. Marc and Ann's life at their farm closely resembles the way that I grew up, with family music and food anchored in regional traditions always at the center of important activities.

My grandfather Fred Ronstadt's careful instructions for building a wagon or buggy were found in his papers after he died: how to bend the wood, work the metal on a forge, the finishing details executed in fine woodwork. Also, there is a description of his experiences "on the road," traveling with the

Club Filarmónico Tucsonense to Los Angeles to play concerts in the late 1890s. Marc's meticulous notes describing how an Acadian accordion is assembled, what he had to learn to know how to make one, and exactly why it produces an instrument that plays better than one made by a machine are fascinating and very similar in tone to what my grandfather wrote more than a century ago.

Ann invited me to sing on *Evangeline Made,* a record she produced that featured contemporary artists singing traditional Cajun songs. She flew to Arizona, where I had moved to raise my two children, and we recorded together, with Ann coaching me on the French lyrics. Recording a project of our own was a natural outgrowth of our warm friendship. We'd both had careers screaming over loud bands, and wanted to do something quiet and contemplative. We wanted to sing about the passions of mature women: love and concern for our children, love between trusted and treasured friends, the precariousness of romantic love, the difference between the love you give to the living and the love you give to the dead, the bitterness of a lost love remembered, and the long, steady love you keep for good.

For our album, *Adieu False Heart,* much of which we recorded at the Savoy's farm in Louisiana, Ann presented a great collection of song suggestions. We picked the ones that made us feel like we would die if we didn't get to sing them. We listened to Fiddlin' Arthur Smith's uptempo version of "Adieu False Heart," slowed it down, and changed it to a minor key and a modal scale. We resolved to record only traditional songs, and then sang "Walk Away Renee," the pop hit we remembered from the sixties. Ann found "Marie Mouri," a Cajun song based on a poem written by a slave in the eighteenth century, and "Parlez-moi d'amour," a song of heartbreaking sentiment that had been popular in Paris between the two world wars. We hung out in our pajamas and rehearsed the harmonies, shared stories about our lives and children, and drank pots of black tea and Marc's incredibly strong coffee. When we finished rehearsing or re-cording for the day, we would sit outside in front of a fire that Marc fed with logs the size of boulders, and stare through the trees at the moon or the lowering Louisiana sky.

Someone once asked me why people sing. I answered that they sing for many of the same reasons the birds sing. They sing for a mate, to claim their territory, or simply to give voice to the delight of being alive in the midst of a beautiful day. Perhaps more than the birds do, humans hold a grudge. They sing to complain of how grievously they have been wronged, and how to avoid it in the future. They sing to help themselves execute a job of work. They sing so the subsequent generations won't forget what the current generation endured, or dreamed, or delighted in.

The essential elements of singing are voice, musicianship, and story. It is the rare artist who has all three in abundance.

Because of the wonder of YouTube, I was able to reconnect to the singing of Pastora Pavón, the voice I heard rising from the 78 rpm recordings owned by my father when I was three. Known as La Niña de los Peines, or the girl with the combs, she is viewed, in the long lens of history, to be among the great-est flamenco singers Spain has ever produced. It was a thrill to hear that voice again after some sixty years, and interesting to examine the elements of a great voice that was able to affect me so strongly as a small child *and* as an experienced singer later in life. What is it that makes her singing inimitable, searing, and able to leap cultural and language barriers while she addresses the most essential yearnings and expectations of humankind? What is it that she shares with her other European singing sisters, Yanka Rupkina of Bulgaria, Amália Rodrigues of Portugal, Edith Piaf of France, singers who can make me feel like they have grabbed me by the throat and told me, urgently, that I *must* listen to something they have to tell me, even when it's in a language I don't understand? I don't know the answer.

I sang my last concert on November 7, 2009, at the Brady Memorial Auditorium in San Antonio. I was performing with my beloved Mariachi Los Camperos, and a wonderful folkloric dance troupe, Ballet Folklorico Paso del Norte. My old roommate Adam Mitchell, an enthusiastic fan of the Camperos, was in the audience. After the show, we went back to my hotel to laugh and reminisce about our Malibu days and how carefree they seemed compared to our mature lives, with children and responsibilities that we could only vaguely imagine in our precipitous youth. Adam felt that of all the bands I had toured with, some were as good as, but none surpassed, the Camperos. He also felt, in the times that he had heard me perform with a still-healthy voice, he had never seen me as happy or relaxed in any performances as I was while singing the Mexican shows. I agreed.

Epilogue

I LIVE THESE DAYS with my two children, and am watching them navigate the wonderful and strange passage from teenager to young adult. They both play instruments, have a lively and active interest in music, and use it to process their feelings in a private setting. This is the fundamental value of music, and I feel sorry for a culture that depends too much on delegating its musical expression to professionals. It is fine to have heroes, but we should do our own singing first, even if it is never heard beyond the shower curtain.

My father died at home in 1995, with all four of his children at his bedside. In the forty-eight hours before he died, he recited a twenty-verse limerick from memory, sang us a beautiful Mexican song, "Collar de Perlas," and read us funny passages from the book he was reading, Gabriel García Márquez's *Love in the Time of Cholera*. At some point he put down the book and devoted his entire attention to the strange work of dying. He faced it with great courage. It changed the way I feel about death. While I don't exactly embrace it, I no longer fear it in the same way.

In Tucson, my sister, brothers, and cousins assemble on the third Sunday of every month to eat great food and sing the old family songs. My cousins John and Bill Ronstadt play regularly in musical establishments in Tucson. My brother Michael tours the United States, Mexico, Canada, and the British Isles with his group Ronstadt Generations, performing original material and traditional songs of the Southwest. In addition to my brother, the group includes his two sons, Mikey, who sings and plays the cello, and Petie, who sings and plays bass and guitar. My beautiful cousin Britt Ronstadt sings in several rock bands in Tucson, and there is always a line around the block to hear her when she is performing. At nineteen, my niece Mindy Ronstadt, another local Tucson performer, recorded a duet with me in Spanish, "Y Ándale," that was a hit in Mexico. My sister's son, Quico, writes songs and performs. My cousin Bobby George and his wife, Susie, sing in a vocal group with my old Stone Poneys bandmate Bobby Kimmel, who moved back to Tucson. My two brothers and my sister, plus cousins Bill and John, have sung backup on several of my recordings, and I could always rely on their genes to supply the family vocal blend.

People ask me why my career consisted of such rampant eclecticism, and why I didn't simply stick to one type of music. The answer is that when I admire something tremendously, it is difficult not to try to emulate it. Some of the attempts were successful, others not. The only rule I imposed on myself, consciously or unconsciously, was to not try singing something that I hadn't heard in the family living room before the age of ten. If I hadn't heard it by then, I couldn't attempt it with even a shred of authenticity.

At the time, struggling with so many different kinds of music seemed like a complicated fantasy, but from the vantage point of my sixty-seven years, I see it was only a simple dream.

Acknowledgments

A number of people provided assistance to me in the process of assembling this memoir, and I would like to express my gratitude.

John Boylan, my friend, colleague, and fellow road warrior, has been a lot of help both in general and in particular since I met him in 1971. A consummate problem solver, John provided his excellent memory of the many times we shared, acted as research assistant, helped assemble photos, and was chief encourager and computer Sherpa. His support was indispensable.

My assistant, Janet Stark, who is the nicest person I have ever known and one of the most capable, read what I wrote on a daily basis and kept the rest of my life running smoothly so I could have a quiet place to unscramble my thoughts.

John Rockwell has been both friend and mentor to me since the early seventies, and long ago suggested that I might be able to write a coherent sentence. As this is my first attempt at doing so, I hope I don't prove him wrong.

My editor at Simon & Schuster, Jonathan Karp, gave me invaluable encouragement and feedback. He also suggested through the elegant prose of his e-mails that I could write about people instead of every horse I knew and loved. Even though I feel somewhat guilty about leaving Gilliana, Mischief, Sugar Britches, Blue, Africa, and Valentine out of my story, I know that he was right about that and many other things.

Copy editor Philip Bashe did such a meticulous job correcting my flagging memory, appalling punctuation, and garbled syntax that I am red-faced and humbled. I wish I could run this sentence by him. From this day forward I will strongly attempt to place the adverb after the verb.

Acknowledgments

My agent, Steve Wasserman, gave me clear-eyed advice and galvanizing encouragement. I am both flattered and grateful that he agreed to represent me.

John Kosh has provided the design for twenty-one of my album covers, including three that won Grammys for best design, and has done his usual immaculate work for this project. He also endured days of my obsessing about font style without blocking me from his e-mail. My admiration, appreciation, and love for him is boundless.

Sam Sargent helped edit and process photos.

Mary Clementine provided hugs and encouragement. Team members: Peter Paterno, Wally Franson, Sue Ollweiler, and Carla Sheppard.

Finally, early readers who gave much-appreciated feedback include Lawrence Downes, Rick Kott, Sydney Goldstein, Peter Asher, Katherine Orloff, Virginia Baker, Wendy Brigode, Cathy Patrick, Wyatt Wade, and Jet Thomas.

Discography

1. THE STONE PONEYS — *THE STONE PONEYS* — CAPITOL — JANUARY 1967

Produced by Nik Venet

Sweet Summer Blue and Gold (B. Kimmel–K. Edwards)
If I Were You (B. Kimmel–K. Edwards)
Just a Little Bit of Rain (Fred Neil)
Bicycle Song (Soon Now) (B. Kimmel–K. Edwards)
Orion (Tom Campbell)
Wild About My Lovin' (Adapted by B. Kimmel–L. Ronstadt–K. Edwards)
Back Home (Ken Edwards)
Meredith (On My Mind) (B. Kimmel–K. Edwards)
Train and the River (B. Kimmel–K. Edwards)
All the Beautiful Things (B. Kimmel–K. Edwards)
2:10 Train (Tom Campbell–Linda Albertano)

2. THE STONE PONEYS — *EVERGREEN, VOL. 2* — CAPITOL — JUNE 1967

Produced by Nik Venet

December Dream (John Braheny)
Song About the Rain (Steve Gillette)
Autumn Afternoon (K. Edwards–B. Kimmel)
I've Got to Know (Pamela Polland)
Evergreen Part One (K. Edwards–B. Kimmel)
Evergreen Part Two (K. Edwards–B. Kimmel)
Different Drum (Mike Nesmith)
Driftin' (K. Edwards–B. Kimmel)
One for One (Al Silverman–Austin DeLone)
Back on the Street Again (Steve Gillette)

Toys in Time (K. Edwards–B. Kimmel)
New Hard Times (M. Smith–B. Kimmel)

3. LINDA RONSTADT — *THE STONE PONEYS AND FRIENDS, VOL. III* — CAPITOL — APRIL 1968

Produced by Nik Venet

Fragments:
Golden Song (Steve Gillette)
Merry-Go-Round (Tom Campbell)
Love Is a Child (Steve Gillette)
By the Fruits of Their Labor (Robert Kimmel–Ken Edwards)
Hobo (Tim Buckley)
Star and a Stone (Robert Kimmel–Ken Edwards)
Let's Get Together (Chet Powers)
Up to My Neck in High Muddy Water (Wakefield–Herald–Yellin)
Aren't You the Girl? (Tim Buckley)
Wings (Tim Buckley)
Some of Shelly's Blues (Mike Nesmith)
Stoney End (Laura Nyro)

4. LINDA RONSTADT — *HAND SOWN . . . HOME GROWN* — CAPITOL — MARCH 1969

Produced by Chip Douglas

Baby You've Been on My Mind (Bob Dylan)
Silver Threads and Golden Needles (J. Rhodes–D. Reynolds)
Bet No One Ever Hurt This Bad (Randy Newman)
A Number and a Name (S. Gillette–T. Campbell)
The Only Mama That'll Walk the Line (Ivy J. Bryant–Earl Ball)
The Long Way Around (Ken Edwards)
Break My Mind (John D. Loudermilk)
I'll Be Your Baby Tonight (Bob Dylan)
It's About Time (Chip Douglas)
We Need a Whole Lot More of Jesus (And a Lot Less Rock & Roll)
    (Wayne Raney)
The Dolphins (Fred Neil)

5. LINDA RONSTADT — *SILK PURSE* — CAPITOL — MARCH 1970

Produced by Elliot Mazer

Lovesick Blues (Irving Mills–C. Friend)
Are My Thoughts with You? (Mickey Newbury)
Will You Love Me Tomorrow (Gerry Goffin–Carole King)
Nobody's (Gary White)
Louise (Paul Siebel)
Long Long Time (Gary White)
Mental Revenge (Mel Tillis)
I'm Leavin' It All Up to You (D. Terry Jr.–D. Harris)
He Darked the Sun (Bernie Leadon–Gene Clark)
Life Is Like a Mountain Railway (Trad. arr. E. Mazer–L. Ronstadt)

6. LINDA RONSTADT — *LINDA RONSTADT* — CAPITOL — JANUARY 1972

Produced by John Boylan

Rock Me on the Water (Jackson Browne)
Crazy Arms (R. Mooney–C. Seals)
I Won't Be Hangin' Round (Eric Kaz)
I Still Miss Someone (Johnny Cash–Roy Cash)
In My Reply (Livingston Taylor)
I Fall to Pieces (Hank Cochran–Harlan Howard)
Ramblin' 'Round (Woody Guthrie–Huddie Ledbetter–
    John Lomax)
Birds (Neil Young)
I Ain't Always Been Faithful (Eric Andersen)
Rescue Me (W. C. Smith, R. Miner)

7. LINDA RONSTADT — *DON'T CRY NOW* — ASYLUM — SEPTEMBER 1973

Produced by Peter Asher, John Boylan, and John David Souther

I Can Almost See It (J. D. Souther)
Love Has No Pride (Eric Kaz–Libby Titus)

Silver Threads and Golden Needles (J. Rhodes–D. Reynolds)

Desperado (Don Henley–Glenn Frey)

Don't Cry Now (J. D. Souther)

Sail Away (Randy Newman)

Colorado (Rick Roberts)

The Fast One (J. D. Souther)

Everybody Loves a Winner (Bill Williams–Booker T. Jones)

I Believe in You (Neil Young)

8. LINDA RONSTADT — *HEART LIKE A WHEEL* — CAPITOL — NOVEMBER 1974

Produced by Peter Asher

You're No Good (Clint Ballard Jr.)

It Doesn't Matter Anymore (Paul Anka)

Faithless Love (J. D. Souther)

The Dark End of the Street (Dan Pennington–Wayne Moman)

Heart Like a Wheel (Anna McGarrigle)

When Will I Be Loved (Phil Everly)

Willin' (Lowell George)

I Can't Help It (If I'm Still In Love With You) (Hank Williams)

Keep Me From Blowing Away (Paul Craft)

You Can Close Your Eyes (James Taylor)

9. LINDA RONSTADT — *PRISONER IN DISGUISE* — ASYLUM — SEPTEMBER 1975

Produced by Peter Asher

Love Is a Rose (Neil Young)

Hey Mister, That's Me Up on the Jukebox (James Taylor)

Roll Um Easy (Lowell George)

The Tracks of My Tears (William Robinson–Marv Tarplin–Warren
   Moore)

Prisoner in Disguise (John David Souther)

Heat Wave (Holland–Dozier–Holland)

Many Rivers to Cross (Jimmy Cliff)

The Sweetest Gift (with Emmylou Harris) (J. B. Coats)
You Tell Me That I'm Falling Down (Anna McGarrigle–C. S. Holland)
I Will Always Love You (Dolly Parton)
Silver Blue (John David Souther)

10. LINDA RONSTADT—*HASTEN DOWN THE WIND*—ASYLUM— AUGUST 1976

Produced by Peter Asher

Lose Again (Karla Bonoff)
The Tattler (Ry Cooder–Russ Titelman–Washington Phillips)
If He's Ever Near (Karla Bonoff)
That'll Be the Day (J. Allison–Buddy Holly–Norman Petty)
Lo Siento Mi Vida (Linda Ronstadt–Kenny Edwards–Gilbert Ronstadt)
Hasten Down the Wind (Warren Zevon)
Rivers of Babylon (B. Dowe–S. McNaughton)
Give One Heart (John and Johanna Hall)
Try Me Again (Linda Ronstadt–Andrew Gold)
Crazy (Willie Nelson)
Down So Low (Tracy Nelson)
Someone to Lay Down Beside Me (Karla Bonoff)

11. LINDA RONSTADT—*SIMPLE DREAMS*—ASYLUM— AUGUST 1977

Produced by Peter Asher

It's So Easy (Buddy Holly–Norman Petty)
Carmelita (Warren Zevon)
Simple Man, Simple Dream (J. D. Souther)
Sorrow Lives Here (Eric Kaz)
I Never Will Marry (Trad. arr. by Linda Ronstadt)
Blue Bayou (Roy Orbison–Joe Melson)
Poor Poor Pitiful Me (Warren Zevon)
Maybe I'm Right (Robert Wachtel)
Tumbling Dice (Mick Jagger–Keith Richards)
Old Paint (Trad. arr. by Linda Ronstadt)

12. LINDA RONSTADT—*LIVING IN THE U.S.A.*—ASYLUM—SEPTEMBER 1978

Produced by Peter Asher

Back in the U.S.A. (Chuck Berry)
When I Grow Too Old to Dream (Oscar Hammerstein II–
  Sigmund Romberg)
Just One Look (G. Carrol–D. Payne)
Alison (Elvis Costello)
White Rhythm and Blues (J. D. Souther)
All That You Dream (Paul Barrere–Bill Payne)
Ooh Baby Baby (William Robinson–Warren Moore)
Mohammed's Radio (Warren Zevon)
Blowing Away (Eric Kaz)
Love Me Tender (Elvis Presley–Vera Matson)

13. LINDA RONSTADT—*MAD LOVE*—ASYLUM—FEBRUARY 1980

Produced by Peter Asher

Mad Love (Mark Goldenberg)
Party Girl (Elvis Costello)
How Do I Make You (Billy Steinberg)
I Can't Let Go (Chip Taylor–Al Gorgoni)
Hurt So Bad (Teddy Randazzo–Bobby Wilding–Bobby Hart)
Look Out For My Love (Neil Young)
Cost of Love (Mark Goldenberg)
Justine (Mark Goldenberg)
Girls Talk (Elvis Costello)
Talking in the Dark (Elvis Costello)

14. LINDA RONSTADT—*GET CLOSER*—ASYLUM—SEPTEMBER 1982

Produced by Peter Asher

Get Closer (Jonathan Carroll)
The Moon Is a Harsh Mistress (Jimmy Webb)

I Knew You When (Joe South)
Easy for You to Say (Jimmy Webb)
People Gonna Talk (William Wheeler–Lee Dorsey–Morris Levy–
    Clarence L. Lewis)
Talk to Me of Mendocino (Kate McGarrigle)
I Think It's Gonna Work Out Fine (with James Taylor)
    (Rose Marie McCoy–Sylvia McKinney)
Mr. Radio (Roderick Taylor)
Lies (Buddy Randell–Beau Charles)
Tell Him (Bert Russell)
Sometimes You Just Can't Win (with John David Souther)
    (Smokey Stover)
My Blue Tears (with Dolly Parton and Emmylou Harris) (Dolly Parton)

15. LINDA RONSTADT — *WHAT'S NEW* — ASYLUM — SEPTEMBER 1983

Produced by Peter Asher

What's New? (Johnny Burke–Bob Haggart)
I've Got a Crush on You (George Gershwin–Ira Gershwin)
Guess I'll Hang My Tears Out to Dry (Sammy Cahn–Jule Styne)
Crazy He Calls Me (Carl Sigman–Sidney Keith Russell)
Someone to Watch Over Me (George Gershwin–Ira Gershwin)
I Don't Stand a Ghost of a Chance With You (Bing Crosby–Ned
    Washington–Victor Young)
What'll I Do? (Irving Berlin)
Lover Man (Oh Where Can You Be?) (Jimmy Davis–Jimmy Sherman–
    Roger "Ram" Ramirez)
Good-bye (Gordon Jenkins)

16. LINDA RONSTADT — *LUSH LIFE* — ASYLUM — NOVEMBER 1984

Produced by Peter Asher

When I Fall in Love (Edward Heyman–Victor Young)
Skylark (Hoagy Carmichael–Johnny Mercer)
It Never Entered My Mind (Lorenz Hart–Richard Rodgers)
Mean to Me (Fred Ahlert–Roy Turk)

When Your Lover Has Gone (Einar Swan)
I'm a Fool to Want You (J. Herron–F. Sinatra–J. Wolf)
You Took Advantage of Me (Lorenz Hart–Richard Rodgers)
Sophisticated Lady (D. Ellington–I. Mills–M. Parrish)
Can't We Be Friends (P. James–K. Swift)
My Old Flame (Sam Coslow–Arthur Johnston)
Falling in Love Again (Frederick Hollander–Sammy Lerner)
Lush Life (Billy Strayhorn)

17. LINDA RONSTADT—*FOR SENTIMENTAL REASONS*— ASYLUM—SEPTEMBER 1986

Produced by Peter Asher

When You Wish Upon a Star (Ned Washington–Leigh Harline)
Bewitched, Bothered and Bewildered (Lorenz Hart–Richard Rodgers)
You Go to My Head (Haven Gillespie–Joe Fred Coots)
But Not for Me (Ira Gershwin–George Gershwin)
My Funny Valentine (Lorenz Hart–Richard Rodgers)
I Get Along Without You Very Well (Hoagy Carmichael)
Am I Blue (Grant Clarke–Harry Akst)
(I Love You) For Sentimental Reasons (Deek Watson–William Best)
Straighten Up and Fly Right (Nat King Cole–Irving Mills)
Little Girl Blue (Lorenz Hart–Richard Rodgers)
'Round Midnight (Bernie Hanighen–Cootie Williams–
    Thelonious Monk)

18. LINDA RONSTADT, EMMYLOU HARRIS, AND DOLLY PARTON—*TRIO*—WARNER BROS.—MARCH 1987

Produced by George Massenburg

The Pain of Loving You (Dolly Parton–Porter Wagoner)
Making Plans (Johnny Russell–Voni Morrison)
To Know Him Is to Love Him (Phil Spector)
Hobo's Meditation (Jimmie Rodgers)
Wildflowers (Dolly Parton)
Telling Me Lies (Linda Thompson–Betsy Cook)
My Dear Companion (Jean Ritchie)

Those Memories of You (Alan O'Bryant)
I've Had Enough (Kate McGarrigle)
Rosewood Casket (Trad.)
Farther Along (Trad.)

19. LINDA RONSTADT — *CANCIONES DE MI PADRE* — ASYLUM — SEPTEMBER 1987

Produced by Peter Asher and Rubén Fuentes

Por Un Amor (Gilberto Parra)
Los Laureles (José López)
Hay Unos Ojos (Rubén Fuentes)
La Cigarra (Ray Pérez Y Soto)
Tú Sólo Tú (Felipe Valdez Leal)
Y Ándale (Minerva Elizondo)
Rogaciano El Huapanguero (Valeriano Trejo)
La Charreada (Felipe Bermejo)
Dos Arbolitos (Chucho Martinez Gil)
Corrido de Cananea (Rubén Fuentes)
La Barca de Guaymas (Rubén Fuentes)
La Calandria (Nicandro Castillo)
El Sol Que Tú Eres (Daniel Valdez)

20. LINDA RONSTADT — *CRY LIKE A RAINSTORM, HOWL LIKE THE WIND* — ASYLUM — SEPTEMBER 1989

Produced by Peter Asher

Still Within the Sound of My Voice (Jimmy Webb)
Cry Like a Rainstorm (Eric Kaz)
All My Life (with Aaron Neville) (Karla Bonoff)
I Need You (with Aaron Neville) (Paul Carrack–Nick Lowe–
    Martin Belmont)
Adios (Jimmy Webb)
Trouble Again (Karla Bonoff)
I Keep It Hid (Jimmy Webb)
So Right, So Wrong (Paul Carrack–Nick Lowe–Martin Belmont)
Shattered (Jimmy Webb)

When Something Is Wrong with My Baby (with Aaron Neville) (Isaac
  Hayes–David Porter)
Goodbye My Friend (Karla Bonoff)

21. LINDA RONSTADT—*MAS CANCIONES*—ASYLUM— OCTOBER 1991

Produced by George Massenburg and Rubén Fuentes

Ta Ta Dios (Valeriano Trejo)
El Toro Relajo (Felipe Bermejo)
Mi Ranchito (Felipe Valdés Leal)
La Mariquita (Rubén Fuentes)
Gritenme Piedras del Campo (Cuco Sanchez)
Siempre Hace Frio (Cuco Sanchez)
El Crucifijo de Piedra (Antonio y Roberto Cantoral)
Palomita de Ojos Negros (Tomas Mendez)
Pena de Los Amores (Jose Luis Almada)
El Camino (Jesus Navarro)
El Gustito (Jose Lopez)
El Sueño (Nicandro Castillo)

22. LINDA RONSTADT—*FRENESÍ*—ASYLUM—NOVEMBER 1992

Produced by Peter Asher and George Massenburg

Frenesí (Alberto Dominguez)
Mentira Salomé (Ignacio Pinero)
Alma Adentro (Sylvia Rexach)
Entre Abismos (Victor Manuel Matos)
Cuando Me Querías Tú (Emilio Catarell Vela)
Piel Canela (Bobby Capo)
Verdad Amarga (Consuelo Velazquez)
Despojos (Francisco Arrieta)
En Mi Soledad (Miguel Pous)
Piensa En Mí (Agustin Lara)
Quiéreme Mucho (Gonzalo Roig–Agustin Rodriguez)
Perfidia (Alberto Dominguez)
Te Quiero Dijiste (Maria Grever)

23. LINDA RONSTADT— *WINTER LIGHT*— ASYLUM— NOVEMBER 1993

Produced by George Massenburg and Linda Ronstadt

Heartbeats Accelerating (Anna McGarrigle)
Do What You Gotta Do (Jimmy Webb)
Anyone Who Had a Heart (Burt Bacharach–Hal David)
Don't Talk (Put Your Head on My Shoulder) (B. Wilson–A. Asher)
Oh No Not My Baby (Gerry Goffin–Carole King)
It's Too Soon to Know (Deborah Chessler)
I Just Don't Know What to Do with Myself (Burt Bacharach–Hal David)
A River for Him (Emmylou Harris)
Adónde Voy (Tish Hinojosa)
You Can't Treat the Wrong Man Right (Jimmy Webb)
Winter Light (Zbigniew Preisner–Eric Kaz–Linda Ronstadt)

24. LINDA RONSTADT— *FEELS LIKE HOME*— ASYLUM— APRIL 1995

Produced by George Massenburg and Linda Ronstadt

The Waiting (Tom Petty)
Walk On (Matraca Berg–Ronnie Samoset)
High Sierra (Harley L. Allen)
After the Gold Rush (Neil Young)
The Blue Train (Jennifer Kimball–Tom Kimmel)
Feels Like Home (Randy Newman)
Teardrops Will Fall (E. V. Deane)
Morning Blues (Trad. arr. by Auldridge–Gaudreau–Coleman–Klein)
Women 'Cross the River (David Olney)
Lover's Return (A. P. Carter)

25. LINDA RONSTADT— *DEDICATED TO THE ONE I LOVE*— ELEKTRA— JUNE 1996

Produced by George Massenburg and Linda Ronstadt

Dedicated to the One I Love (Lowman Pauling–Ralph Bass)
Be My Baby (Phil Spector–Jeff Barry–Ellie Greenwich)

In My Room (Brian Wilson–Gary Usher)
Devoted to You (Boudleaux Bryant)
Baby I Love You (Phil Spector–Jeff Barry–Ellie Greenwich)
Devoted to You (instrumental) (Boudleaux Bryant)
Angel Baby (Rosalie Hamlin)
We Will Rock You (Brian May)
Winter Light (Zbigniew Preisner–Eric Kaz–Linda Ronstadt)
Brahms' Lullaby (Johannes Brahms)
Good Night (John Lennon–Paul McCartney)

26. LINDA RONSTADT — *WE RAN* — ELEKTRA — JUNE 1998

Produced by Glyn Johns, with George Massenburg, Peter Asher, Linda Ronstadt, and Waddy Wachtel

When We Ran (John Hiatt)
If I Should Fall Behind (Bruce Springsteen)
Give Me a Reason (M. Hall)
Ruler of My Heart (Naomi Neville)
Just Like Tom Thumb's Blues (Bob Dylan)
Cry Till My Tears Run Dry (Doc Pomus)
I Go to Pieces (Waddy Wachtel–Troy Newman)
Heartbreak Kind (Marty Stuart–Paul Kennerley)
Damage (Waddy Wachtel)
Icy Blue Heart (John Hiatt)
Dreams of the San Joaquin (Jack Wesley Routh–Randy Sharp)

27. LINDA RONSTADT, EMMYLOU HARRIS, AND DOLLY PARTON — *TRIO II* — WARNER BROS. — FEBRUARY 9, 1999

Produced by George Massenburg

Lover's Return (A. P. Carter)
High Sierra (Harley L. Allen)
Do I Ever Cross Your Mind (Dolly Parton)
After the Gold Rush (Neil Young)
The Blue Train (Jennifer Kimball–Tom Kimmel)
I Feel the Blues Movin' In (Del McCoury)
You'll Never Be the Sun (Donagh Long)

He Rode All the Way to Texas (John Starling)

Feels Like Home (Randy Newman)

When We're Gone, Long Gone (Kieran Kane–Paul O'Hara)

28. LINDA RONSTADT AND EMMYLOU HARRIS – *WESTERN WALL: THE TUCSON SESSIONS* – ELEKTRA – AUGUST 24, 1999

Produced by Glyn Johns

Loving the Highway Man (Andy Prieboy)

Raise the Dead (Emmylou Harris)

For a Dancer (Jackson Browne)

Western Wall (Rosanne Cash)

1917 (David Olney)

He Was Mine (Paul Kennerley)

Sweet Spot (Emmylou Harris–Jill Cunniff)

Sisters of Mercy (Leonard Cohen)

Falling Down (Patty Griffin)

Valerie (Patti Scialfa)

This Is to Mother You (Sinead O'Connor)

All I Left Behind (Emmylou Harris–Kate and Anna McGarrigle)

Across the Border (Bruce Springsteen)

29. LINDA RONSTADT – *A MERRY LITTLE CHRISTMAS* – ELEKTRA – OCTOBER 10, 2000

Produced by John Boylan and George Massenburg

The Christmas Song (Mel Tormé–Robert Wells)

I'll Be Home for Christmas (Walter Kent–Kim Gannon)

White Christmas (Irving Berlin)

Have Yourself a Merry Little Christmas (Hugh Martin–Ralph Blane)

O Come, O Come, Emmanuel (Trad.)

Xicochi, Xicochi (Gaspar Fernandez)

I Wonder as I Wander (John Jacob Niles)

Away In a Manger (Trad.)

Lo, How a Rose E're Blooming (Trad.)

Welsh Carol (Trad.)

Past Three O'clock (Trad.)

O Magnum Mysterium (Tomás Luis de Victoria)
Silent Night (Josef Mohr–Franz Xaver Gruber)

30. LINDA RONSTADT—*HUMMIN' TO MYSELF*—VERVE—NOVEMBER 9, 2004

Produced by John Boylan and George Massenburg

Tell Him I Said Hello (Jack J. Canning–Bill Hegner)
Never Will I Marry (Frank Loesser)
Cry Me a River (Arthur Hamilton)
Hummin' to Myself (Sammy Fain–Herbert Magidson–Monty Siegel)
Miss Otis Regrets (Cole Porter)
I Fall in Love Too Easily (Sammy Cahn–Jule Styne)
Blue Prelude (Joe Bishop–Gordon Jenkins)
Day Dream (Duke Ellington–John Latouche–Billy Strayhorn)
I've Never Been in Love Before (Frank Loesser)
Get Out of Town (Cole Porter)
I'll Be Seeing You (Sammy Fain–Irving Kahal)

31. LINDA RONSTADT AND ANN SAVOY (THE ZOZO SISTERS)—*ADIEU FALSE HEART*—VANGUARD—JULY 25, 2006

Produced by Steve Buckingham

Adieu False Heart (Trad.)
I Can't Get Over You (Julie Miller)
Marie Mouri (David Greely)
King of Bohemia (Richard Thompson)
Tournes, Tournes Bébé Créole (Michael Hindenoch)
Go Away from My Window (John Jacob Niles)
Burns Supper (Richard Thompson)
The One I Love Is Gone (Bill Monroe)
Rattle My Cage (Chas Justus)
Parlez-Moi d'Amour (J. Neuberger)
Too Old to Die Young (Scott Dooley–John Hadley–Kevin Welch)
Walk Away Renee (Mike Brown–Bob Calilli–Tony Sansone)

COMPILATION ALBUMS:

1. LINDA RONSTADT — *DIFFERENT DRUM* — CAPITOL — 1974

Different Drum
Rock Me on the Water
I'll Be Your Baby Tonight
Hobo
Stoney End
Long Long Time
Up to My Neck in High Muddy Water
Some of Shelly's Blues
In My Reply
Will You Love Me Tomorrow

2. LINDA RONSTADT — *GREATEST HITS* — ASYLUM — 1976

You're No Good
Silver Threads and Golden Needles
Desperado
Love Is a Rose
That'll Be the Day
Long Long Time
Different Drum
When Will I Be Loved
Love Has No Pride
Heat Wave
It Doesn't Matter Anymore
The Tracks of My Tears

3. LINDA RONSTADT — *A RETROSPECTIVE* — CAPITOL — 1977

When Will I Be Loved
Silver Threads and Golden Needles
Hobo
I Fall to Pieces
Birds
I Can't Help It (If I'm Still In Love With You)

Different Drum
Some of Shelly's Blues
I'll Be Your Baby Tonight
Louise
Long Long Time
Faithless Love
Rock Me on the Water
Lovesick Blues
Rescue Me
Just a Little Bit of Rain
The Long Way Around
You're No Good
Ramblin' 'Round
Crazy Arms
It Doesn't Matter Anymore
Will You Love Me Tomorrow

4. LINDA RONSTADT—*GREATEST HITS VOLUME II*— ASYLUM—1980

It's So Easy
I Can't Let Go
Hurt So Bad
Blue Bayou
How Do I Make You
Back in the U.S.A.
Ooh Baby Baby
Poor Poor Pitiful Me
Tumbling Dice
Just One Look
Someone to Lay Down Beside Me

5. LINDA RONSTADT—*'ROUND MIDNIGHT*—ASYLUM—1986

Disk 1:
What's New
I've Got a Crush on You

Guess I'll Hang My Tears Out to Dry
Crazy He Calls Me
Someone to Watch Over Me
I Don't Stand a Ghost of a Chance
What'll I Do
Lover Man (Oh Where Can You Be)
Good-bye
When I Fall in Love
Skylark
It Never Entered My Mind
Mean to Me
When Your Lover Has Gone
I'm a Fool to Want You

Disk 2:

You Took Advantage of Me
Sophisticated Lady
Can't We Be Friends
My Old Flame
Falling in Love Again
Lush Life
When You Wish Upon a Star
Bewitched, Bothered and Bewildered
You Go to My Head
But Not for Me
My Funny Valentine
I Get Along Without You Very Well
Am I Blue
(I Love You) For Sentimental Reasons
Straighten Up and Fly Right
Little Girl Blue
'Round Midnight

6. LINDA RONSTADT—*HER GREATEST HITS AND FINEST PERFORMANCES*—READER'S DIGEST—1997

Disk 1:

Different Drum
When Will I Be Loved
You're No Good
The Tracks of My Tears
Ooh Baby Baby
Heat Wave
Hurt So Bad
It's So Easy
Long Long Time
Blue Bayou
Love Is a Rose
I Can't Help It (If I'm Still In Love With You)
Silver Threads and Golden Needles
Someone to Lay Down Beside Me
Poor Poor Pitiful Me
Love Me Tender
Crazy
Back in the U.S.A.
Get Closer
That'll Be the Day

Disk 2:

What's New
But Not for Me
Am I Blue
When I Fall in Love
Bewitched, Bothered and Bewildered
You Took Advantage of Me
Someone to Watch Over Me
Lush Life
Straighten Up and Fly Right
What'll I Do
My Funny Valentine
(I Love You) For Sentimental Reasons

When You Wish Upon a Star
Falling in Love Again
Little Girl Blue
Skylark
I've Got a Crush on You
It Never Entered My Mind
Sophisticated Lady
Lover Man (Oh Where Can You Be?)

Disk 3:

Somewhere Out There
All My Life
I Think It's Gonna Work Out Fine
Sometimes You Just Can't Win
Don't Know Much
La Calandria
Telling Me Lies
To Know Him Is to Love Him
My Dear Companion
I've Had Enough
Poor Wandering One
I Want a Horse
Winter Light
When I Grow Too Old to Dream
It Doesn't Matter Anymore
Try Me Again
Desperado
I Keep It Hid
Goodbye My Friend
Adios

7. LINDA RONSTADT — BOX SET — RHINO — 1997

Disk 1:

When We Ran
Ruler of My Heart
Cry Till My Tears Run Dry

We Will Rock You

Winter Light

Anyone Who Had a Heart

I Just Don't Know What to Do with Myself

Don't Talk (Put Your Head on My Shoulder)

Do What You Gotta Do

Heartbeats Accelerating

Goodbye My Friend

Adios

Cry Like a Rainstorm

Trouble Again

Easy for You to Say

The Moon Is a Harsh Mistress

Get Closer

Hurt So Bad

I Can't Let Go

Ooh Baby Baby

Just One Look

Poor Poor Pitiful Me

Disk 2:

Blue Bayou

Try Me Again

Heat Wave

Heart Like a Wheel

It Doesn't Matter Anymore

You're No Good

When Will I Be Loved

Long Long Time

Different Drum

Little Girl Blue

I Get Along Without You Very Well

My Funny Valentine

When You Wish Upon a Star

It Never Entered My Mind

Skylark

What's New

Quiéreme Mucho

Frenesí

Mentira Salome

La Mariquita

El Crucifijo de Piedra

Disk 3:

High Sierra (with Dolly Parton and Emmylou Harris)

Lover's Return (with Dolly Parton and Emmylou Harris)

The Blue Train (with Dolly Parton and Emmylou Harris)

Feels Like Home (with Dolly Parton and Emmylou Harris)

Gentle Annie (with Kate and Anna McGarrigle)

Please Remember Me (with Aaron Neville)

After the Gold Rush (with Valerie Carter and Emmylou Harris)

Moonlight in Vermont (with Frank Sinatra)

El Camino (with Pete and Mike Ronstadt)

All My Life (with Aaron Neville)

Don't Know Much (with Aaron Neville)

Back in the U.S.A. (with Chuck Berry)

El Sol Que Tu Eres (with Danny Valdez)

Telling Me Lies (with Dolly Parton and Emmylou Harris)

Somewhere Out There (with James Ingram)

I Think It's Gonna Work Out Fine (with James Taylor)

I Never Will Marry (with Dolly Parton)

Prisoner in Disguise (with J. D. Souther)

Faithless Love (with J. D. Souther)

I Can't Help It (If I'm Still In Love With You) (with Emmylou Harris)

Disk 4:

Gainesville

Sandman's Coming

My Hero

All I Have to Do Is Dream (with Kermit the Frog)

Dreams to Dream

The Blacksmith

Bandit and a Heartbreaker

Keep Me from Blowing Away

The Sweetest Gift

Freezing

Poor Wandering One

Sorry Her Lot

I Want a Horse

All That You Dream

Hearts Against the Wind

Tumbling Dice

Border Town

Falling Star

Honky Tonk Blues

Lightning Bar Blues

Why

I'd Like to Know

Everybody Has Their Own Ideas

8. LINDA RONSTADT — *THE VERY BEST OF LINDA RONSTADT* — RHINO — 2002

When Will I Be Loved

Heat Wave

You're No Good

It's So Easy

Blue Bayou

Just One Look

Different Drum

Poor Poor Pitiful Me

The Tracks of My Tears

That'll Be the Day

Ooh Baby Baby

Long Long Time

Back in the U.S.A.

Love Is a Rose

Hurt So Bad

Heart Like a Wheel

Adios

Somewhere Out There

Don't Know Much

All My Life
Winter Light

9. LINDA RONSTADT — *JARDÍN AZUL:*
LAS CANCIONES FAVORITAS — RHINO — 2004

La Charreada
Rogaciano el Huapanguero
Cuando Me Querías Tú
Lo Siento mi Vida
Mi Ranchito
La Cigarra
Perfidia (Spanish version)
Siempre Hace Frio
La Mariquita
Quiéreme Mucho
Verdad Amarga
Por Un Amor
El Sol Que Tú Eres
Tata Dios
Adónde Voy
Mentira Salomé
Piel Canela
Hay Unos Ojos
El Sueno
El Crucifijo de Piedra

Index

Page numbers in *italics* refer to illustrations.